THE

Joy *of*
Success

THE
Joy *of*
Success

10 ESSENTIAL SKILLS FOR GETTING THE SUCCESS *YOU* WANT

Susan Ford Collins

WILLIAM MORROW
An Imprint of
HarperCollins*Publishers*

HarperCollins books may be purchased for educational, business, or sales promotional use. For information please write: Special Markets Department, HarperCollins Publishers Inc., 10 East 53rd Street, New York, NY 10022.

FIRST EDITION

Designed by Nicola Ferguson

Printed on acid-free paper

Library of Congress Cataloging-in-Publication Data

Collins, Susan.
The joy of success: 10 essential skills for getting the success *you* want / Susan Ford Collins.—1st ed.
p. cm.
ISBN 0-06-018866-9
1. Success—Psychological aspects. I. Title.
BF37.S8 C544 2003
158.1—dc21   2002026401

03 04 05 06 07 WBC/RRD 10 9 8 7 6 5 4 3 2 1

To my daughters Cathy and Margaret

Because of you, I was able to move past my fears to these skills.
I had to succeed at finding them so you could succeed too—
and you have.

I love you,
Mom

Contents

THE
Joy *of* Success

The Technology
of Success

Afterspending a year researching dysfunction at the National Institute of Mental Health, an idea flashed in my mind. *What if we started studying highly successful people as well?*

The idea incubated quietly for months but then it started waking me at night. I found myself turning on the light to jot down notes. Half-asleep, I heard myself rehearsing what I would say. Finally, during one of our high-powered weekly conferences at work, I raised my hand and stood up. With fire in my eyes, I explained my idea, including the valuable insights such a study could provide. But instead of becoming excited, my colleagues laughed. Red-faced, yet sure that I was onto something big, I vowed to spend the rest of my life studying successful people.

Months later, my husband was offered a position that was too good to refuse and we moved to suburban Philadelphia. With no research opportunities available and two young daughters to mother, I took a job teaching in a middle school in our neighborhood. I felt blown off course at first, but those classroom years allowed me to share workdays and holidays with my girls and gave me time to begin observing highly successful adults, as well as "gifted" kids.

Through an almost incomprehensible maze created by divorce and new responsibilities as a single mother, I was guided by three questions: *What is success? What skills make people successful? And how can these skills be taught?* My route—filled with detours and roadblocks, starts and restarts, conflicting needs and priorities—would turn out to be similar to the routes highly successful people described.

Then came another unexpected turn. A budget crunch eliminated my teaching position and I was laid off. Since a life compatible with my daughters' needs was still a priority, I started a business nearby and hired people to help me. Knowing I would be creating seminars down the road, I began exploring personal and business development trainings. Some of the Success Skills I had been identifying were included but others were not. These trainings helped people clarify their goals. But I observed participants become even more frustrated when they returned to their lives *without all the skills needed to make the changes they now wanted.*

Next an opportunity presented itself. While attending the World Games at the University of Massachusetts, I met Buckminster Fuller, one of the great visionaries of our time, and spelled out my quest to him. I asked what he thought had made him successful. And, like so many of the people I would interview, after suggesting a few possibilities, he said he wasn't sure. But he was eager to know what I discovered and applauded my "spunk." Then Bucky introduced me to people in other fields, and they introduced me to others.

Since those days at the National Institute of Mental Health, I have shadowed (spent days, weeks, and even months observing) people in practically every field—businesspeople, coaches, athletes, teachers, parents, artists, musicians, writers, entertainers, creators, and inventors. As I studied their work strategies, leadership styles, decision-making processes, relaxation preferences, family and personal lives, month after month, year after year, the same ten skills kept showing up. I decided to call this skill set *The Technology of Success.*

How Can Success Skills Be Taught?

began designing and facilitating *The Technology of Success* public seminars. Weekend after weekend, group after group, each skill seemed to lead to the next. The process flowed naturally from Skill 1 to Skill 10. Some participants knew some of them. Others knew them all but found they had been using them inappropriately. For weeks, months, and years afterward, I received calls from grateful participants who were eager to share successes they were having, triumphs large and small they had only dreamed of until then—jobs found, relationships enjoyed, exams passed, houses bought, products invented, self-confidence and aliveness renewed.

As employers started noticing significant improvements in these employees' attitudes and performances, major corporations—Coopers and Lybrand, American Express, Florida Power and Light, Digital, IBM, Ryder System, Dow Chemical, Kimberly-Clark and Upjohn—invited me to teach *The Technology of Success* in-house. These participants introduced me to others who were happy to have me scrutinize what they did and when and how they did it.

The more people I observed, the more clearly an intriguing dichotomy emerged. All these people were highly successful in their organizations and fields, and some had created followers and successors, but many were overburdened because they couldn't find "anyone smart enough" to replace them. Why could some people share their abilities and understandings while others could not?

The latter group's stories of frustration followed a pattern. After years of start-up, building the right team, fine-tuning the market, and honing a competitive edge, they wanted to slow down. But without successors they were stuck. Sometimes they picked the wrong people, expected too much, stepped in and took over, or just lost their cool. As successful as they were, these people couldn't *pass on* their success.

After fifteen years of conducting corporate workshops, I had an experience that altered the course of my work once again. I received a call from a director at The Upjohn Company asking me to speak at their Regional Sales Conference: "We'll be honoring your daughter Margaret as our Top Sales Representative. When I asked Margaret what her secret was, she said it's the ten Success Skills you taught her. So I want you to teach these skills to the rest of my sales team." Then he asked a favor: "Please don't tell anyone you're her mom until it's over." All during the seminar, Margaret and I passed silently, exchanging furtive winks. Then at the close of the day, excited participants crowded around me until they were asked to take their seats. "Our award winner, Margaret Collins, has something she would like to say." Margaret stood up slowly and pointed her finger at me. "That's my mom." The room fell silent for a moment, and then in one voice roared, "No fair, Margaret—no wonder you won!"

Although Margaret's colleagues shouted those words with good-natured laughter, their "complaint" troubled me. Shouldn't every child have parents who can teach all ten Success Skills? Shouldn't every child have parents who live these skills every day, not just enjoying their own dreams but leading the way for their children to enjoy theirs?

Suddenly I was face-to-face with a realization that had been percolating for months. Most of the participants in my corporate seminars were parents, and many of the questions they asked on breaks were about their children—and their leadership role as parents. The Upjohn group's reaction forced me to realize that, after years of focusing on Corporate America, it was time to expand my model. Here I was teaching these skills in high-profile corporations and government agencies, but I found these skills weren't being taught by parents. Teaching these skills to employees in management was extremely valuable but not nearly as life-changing as it would be if they were learning these skills at home as children, reinforcing them in school, and then bringing them full-blown into the workplace, community, and larger world.

I began reaching farther, speaking in schools and universities, appearing on TV and radio, facilitating conferences and presenting keynotes—American Montessori Society, Independent Teachers, Waldorf Schools, Communities in Schools, and Red Ribbon Campaign/Informed Families—in addition to my corporate work.

The Crisis of Our Time Is Success

Several years ago, I was invited to teach *The Technology of Success* skills to the entire staff of a middle school—administrators, teachers, counselors, PTA members, police, hall aides, and custodians—everyone who had contact with students. I trained teachers and parents, spoke in classrooms and assemblies, and interviewed hundreds of students. At this point I seemed to have come full circle from my middle school classroom days.

I asked each student two questions: "What does success mean to you?" and "What are you doing to get it?" Their answers stunned me. Very few students saw a connection between their future success goals and what they were doing day to day. Those who planned to be music stars were rarely studying music, let alone practicing. Those who expected to be professional athletes were hardly ever on teams or playing ball on corner lots. And most disturbing of all, many students—including ones who came from affluent families—said they didn't want to be successful.

You read that right. More times than I could count, I heard the words *I don't want to be successful.* Why? "Because, if you're successful, you never have time for friends, family, or just fun. You're always working and your boss never appreciates you." These students were deciding their futures by what they saw happening in their parents' lives. Their parents were constantly revving and accelerating to meet new quotas, working harder and longer for bonuses and promotions and to keep up with mortgages and credit cards.

We are experiencing a crisis. We're so productive, competitive, and accessible by cell phone, E-mail, and fax that we rarely have time for the successes we've promised ourselves, the successes that nourish not only our hearts and souls but also the hearts and souls of those we love. How have our lives gotten so out of alignment; how have we gotten so far away from the joy of success?

As satisfying as it has been teaching these ten Success Skills in major corporations, schools, universities, and governments, the outcome I have in mind now is far more enticing and fulfilling. By writing this book, I will be able to share these skills with anyone anywhere who is interested in discovering which things he or she does, amid hectic days and busy evenings, *really matter* and which ones *really don't* and need to be changed.

Thank you to the more than two hundred thousand people who allowed me to explore their lives, thoughts, and emotions in pursuit of these skills. Your names have been changed but the truth of your stories will allow many more people to enjoy what they want far more easily.

Part One

What They Didn't Tell You About Success

THAT YOU NEED TO KNOW *Now*

Escaping the Success Trap

By Learning to

Success File

O ne morning I had an early call from a client who said he had to see me right away. "My life is falling apart—my career and possibly even my marriage." When I met him later, his usually confident voice was cracked and hollow.

Michael and his partners had had quite a run of success, expanding their practice into the sort of waterfront office tower that impressed even them. After years of trying, Michael had finally been able to convince the love of his life to marry him. He had proposed a deal: In exchange for giving up her career and beloved cottage in the woods, she would devote her life to the community service projects she had always wanted to do but never had time for. And he would handle their finances and enjoy the contributions she would make in their name. Accepting his proposal ten years before, Karen had moved to New York.

But this afternoon Michael and his partners made a decision

they had been avoiding for months: Next week they would close their offices to stop the financial hemorrhaging. Tomorrow they would tell their staff. Michael's partners would find work with other groups, but that wasn't what he wanted at this stage in his career. He would stick around to pick up the pieces, renegotiate leases, and possibly stay in business alone. About to tell his wife he might have to renege on their deal, at least temporarily, Michael was distraught.

How could he have done everything "right"—complete a top-notch education, become highly effective and efficient, put in the whatever-it-takes kind of hours that had been demanded of him for years—and have it all turn out "wrong"?

In a matter of minutes, Karen would be pondering the same question as she stood at their kitchen window staring out at the neighborhood she had been working a decade to restore. Tears stung her cheeks as she thought about abandoning the health-assistance program she had been providing schools free of charge, the neighbors she had grown to love as they nailed, hammered, and painted together.

Michael felt successful last week. But today, sitting here with me, he was afraid of sobbing. Michael had accomplished all the successes that had been expected of him. He had jumped through their hoops and over their hurdles, made the requisite amount of money, bought his own home, built a highly regarded practice and sterling reputation. But today he was confronting a new level of reality.

In the process of completing the successes *they*—parents, teachers, bosses, and society—had in mind for him, Michael had neglected the ones he had in mind for himself, the "disapproved of," the "irresponsible," the "selfish," the "too far out." Karen had been pursuing her dreams, doing the community projects she wanted to do, while Michael was pursuing what he thought would give them security. But now that it hadn't, he was rethinking his ideas about success.

The Success Trap: Given All You've Done, Why Aren't You Feeling More Successful?

A s I begin my *Technology of Success* seminars, I ask participants to write down as many successes as they can in the *Success File* I provide. Given a ten-minute time frame, I suggest they start with two hundred successes.

Seminar after seminar, year after year, I was amazed to discover that, despite a lifetime of busy days and finished projects, most participants could recall only fifteen to twenty successes. Successes most often listed were getting good grades; making a team; getting a driver's license; graduating from high school; receiving prizes, trophies, or scholarships; graduating from college or professional training; getting their first job; buying their first car; getting married; renting or buying their own home; meeting quotas; looking good on charts and graphs; earning perks, plaques, and bonuses; receiving promotions and titles; giving birth to their first child.

As I thought about these successes, I began to notice a pattern. These were the successes other people *created* for us. The ones our family and teachers had in mind for us. The ones they believed we should accomplish so Corporate America would hire and promote us. The ones society thought would make us rule-following, hard-working, moneymaking, taxpaying citizens. These were the successes they told us *God* had in mind for us. The ones they taught us to dream.

We remember these successes because other people *managed* our process of achieving them step by step, day to day. They made sure we did our homework and got to school on time. They trained, evaluated, and spelled out the steps we should follow, the results we should produce. And, when we didn't, they provided consequences—disapproval, punishment, restrictions at home, at school, and in our communities. These are the successes they taught us to manage *their* way.

We remember these successes because they went out of their way to *acknowledge* them. Because our parents smiled, shouted "good," "right," or "excellent." Because our teachers praised, promoted, and graduated us. Because our families and friends threw parties and gave us gifts. Because our bosses paid, promoted, perked, and bonused us. Because our marketplace advertised we were "successful" when they issued us a credit card and we started spending regularly, even excessively, on things *they* said would make us feel successful—certain clothes, habits, cars, jewelry, homes, lifestyles, and trips. Bottom line: When we were consuming products *they* wanted us to consume. And paying for them on time. Or, even better for *them*, over time at high interest. These were the successes *they* valued and rewarded.

But you haven't always done what others wanted, far from it. You were no doubt sometimes headstrong or resistant, fearful or insistent on doing things *your* way, on creating experiences they didn't want you to have. And despite punishment and disapproval, anger, upset, lost privileges, you persisted in moving ahead *your way*.

Why didn't you recall those "successes," the ones *they* didn't acknowledge? And *you* didn't acknowledge either? They weren't recognized when you sorted back through memory. They were never labeled as *successes*. In fact, many of your "successes" were filed as "failures"—sometimes significant failures: Failures to follow *their* rules. Failures to want what *they* wanted. Failures to use *their* methods and timings. Failures to live *their* dreams. So millions and millions of your "potential success experiences" now lay dormant in memory, inaccessible and unused. Unenjoyed.

Why is this important now? Because those "unacknowledged successes" are draining energy and reducing your confidence in yourself and your future. Because continuing to depend on other people to acknowledge you means you can't feel successful—*unless they agree. You can't pursue your own dreams and manage them your way.*

Highly successful people have transcended their need to have others create, manage, and acknowledge their successes for them. They have taken over these responsibilities themselves. They are the ones who create their dreams. They are the ones who manage the process day by day, step by step. And they are the ones who acknowledge themselves. This is what you will be learning to do, too, step by step, skill by skill.

Unlocking The Success Trap: Why Is Acknowledgment the First Step?

Acknowledgment *releases* the energy we have invested in a plan, task, or project so it becomes available for what we do next—so that the transaction is *complete.* But we don't just get back the energy we put in, we get back even more, like being paid interest on money we deposit in a bank. That "thank you" or "well done" or "I received it" or "Yeah, I did it" is an essential part of the success process.

Without acknowledgment, we move ahead, but that energy doesn't move ahead with us. Dribs and drabs of your energy are probably tied up here and there. At this point in every seminar someone shares something *unacknowledged* that is still holding him or her back. A parent who never said "I'm proud of you." A friend or mate who never said "I'm sorry." One of the reasons that people stop dreaming is they don't have enough energy left to dream anymore.

Acknowledgment builds confidence. Whenever we encounter new situations, our brains automatically and unconsciously sort through our memories to compare *now* with *then.* If they compare our current situations with past successes, our bodies respond with energy and enthusiasm; we feel optimistic and eager to move ahead. But if our brains compare now with past failures, we feel fearful and anxious. So it behooves each of us to have as many successes in memory as possible. But how?

Success Filing: Self-Acknowledging to Build Momentum and Self-Confidence

As I observed highly successful people, I saw them using a skill I call *Success Filing*. They took time each day to acknowledge the successes they'd had that day. They Success-Filed alone or with people who shared their dreams. Most filed once a day, but some filed more often. Some wrote their successes down on paper, and some simply "wrote" them in memory. They told me they had been Success Filing for years and usually couldn't even remember how they got started.

Instead of *other-confidence*, we must develop *self-confidence*, the confidence it takes to lead ourselves, and others, through the periods of confusion and uncertainty inherent in creating something new, something disagreed with and unaccepted. Something you really want.

Success Filing is the skill you will need to start dreaming again, not little realistic dreams but big, juicy, exciting dreams like those you had as a child, dreams that wake you up in the night excited and propel you out of bed eager for your day.

Here's how to start Success Filing: Pick a time of day that works—on your way home in the car, at dinnertime or bedtime. When and where and who you file with is up to you. What's important is regularity. Imagine rewinding your inner recording to the beginning of your day. Then reexperience it in detail. Notice what you thought, felt, and did when you woke up, when you climbed out of bed . . . moment by moment, thought by thought, action by action until you are back to the same time of day again. What successes did you have today? And what "unacknowledged successes" from your past can you acknowledge as well? Challenge yourself to think of as many as you can, knowing: *When your Success File is full, you feel success-full. When it is low, you feel dependent and needy.*

When you start Success Filing, it helps to write down your successes in a notebook, in a computer file, or on lined paper kept in a file folder. Having this list available on challenging days will be especially valuable as you begin making changes in your life. Eventually Success Filing will become a moment in which you stop to acknowledge yourself and others on the fly.

But what is success? To Success-File, you will need to know.

What Is Success?

B ased on observing highly successful people's lives, I have discovered that success has three essential parts: Success is *completion*—accomplishing what we set out to do, whether a task, a call, an errand, or a dream. Success is *deletion*—knowing when *not* to do, when to say no, when to eliminate habits, methods, or relationships. And success is *creation*—breaking through to solution and innovation and passing on what you've discovered.

I. Success Is Completion

S *uccess is being able to complete what you have in mind:* Getting up early. Lacing your sneakers and running your route. Emptying the trash. Eating a healthy breakfast. Quizzing your child's spelling words. Getting gas in your car. Completing the items you've listed in your time-management system. Following through with salad for lunch instead of your usual pasta. Speaking out about a concern with a project. Stopping by the grocery and dry cleaner on the way home. Reading your child the story you promised. Paying bills. Sharing your day and your mate's. Planning a trip or confirming a reservation. Registering for a class. Reading a book and rethinking your definition of success.

Without daily successes, your life falls apart. Your body gets out of shape. You run out of gas and arrive late for your meeting. Your clients abandon you and find other people to serve them. You never feel heard. Your boss constantly points out your lack of follow-through. There's no food in the refrigerator. Your trash is piling up. There's no clean underwear in the drawer. Your electricity is turned off. Your car isn't running. Your partner is unhappy. Your child is rebellious and untrusting. Insecure.

Without daily successes *your* confidence falls apart, too. *Because completions like these are what the life experience is all about.* Long-term goals are realized in tiny daily steps. Long-term relationships are enjoyed in daily conversations. Long-term careers are the result of day-to-day completions. Long-term dreams come true because you take steps each day with those dreams in mind.

But When Are Enough Completions Enough?

Carly was growing huge tumors in her body. Yes, from the outside, she and her husband seemed to be doing quite well—they had two beautiful children and homes around the world; they had built a multimillion-dollar business and owned their own plane. Little by little the juice had been squeezed out of her life, leaving only pulp. Finally her doctor proposed major surgery. Shocked and repelled, she woke up.

But if she left their business, if she no longer shouldered the responsibilities her husband couldn't, would their business survive? Would her marriage and family stay intact? Originally she had planned to work for ten years, but crisis by crisis she felt compelled to stay longer. With their early goals reached, Carly and her husband had gotten caught in a tailwind that kept pushing them ahead, leaving less and less time for themselves and their children.

Escaping for a few days to a tiny house in the remote mountains of Europe, Carly reconnected with the life she had enjoyed there as a child, spending hours alone in the woods. What had she been thinking and doing differently when her life was rich and fruitful, when she awakened each morning eager for the day, when magic and creativity were daily occurrences? She had been an artist when they met, freewheeling, passionate, and productive, attracting friends wherever she went and talking late into the night. All that remained was a pile of responsibilities she no longer wanted. Sheltered in those ancient stone walls, staring up at the night sky, she remembered who she was and how she wanted to live.

Returning home, Carly was ready to let the pieces fall in healthier places. She drafted a resignation letter and presented it to her husband along with a statement of her new intentions and boundaries. In tears she told him this was the only way she could think of to save their marriage. And shaken, he heard her.

Then instead of taking on the even larger pile of work that had accumulated while she was away, she scheduled a meeting to hand over not just that stack but her title and position as well.

2. Success Is Also Deletion

The *New Webster's Dictionary* says "*Success* is the *accomplishment* of what is *desired or aimed at.*" Yes, that's how most people define success, whether what they desired or aimed at was graduation or retirement, whether what they desired or aimed at was their dream or someone else's.

But that definition contains a potentially fatal flaw. If success can only be accomplishment, then when is enough enough? Has this very definition of success set us up to be "productive robots" always needing to do more and have more: higher scores; higher profits; more exciting sex or adventures; faster cars, planes, bodies, lives. Bigger TVs or ever smaller ones. Higher mountains to climb, deeper space to explore. Always desiring and aiming at, but never there. Never satisfied and successful. Never joyful and whole.

Joy as Oprah Sees It

But the actions of highly successful people often look quite different from *Webster's* definition. Take Oprah Winfrey, for example.

Oprah's personal trainer, Bob Greene, said he used to see a very different Oprah than the one we see on TV. As they headed out for morning workouts, she consistently looked exhausted and flat. Having observed this for some time, he finally asked Oprah: "When was the last time you felt joy?" After taking some time to think back through her memory, Oprah finally replied, "I haven't felt joy in eight years." And to make sure Oprah heard herself, he repeated: "You haven't felt joy in eight years."

One morning soon after, a smiling Oprah greeted him with news: She had just decided to postpone writing her book. He knew what a big decision that had been because Oprah is someone who prides herself on keeping commitments. But this time she had decided *not* to do something she had told herself and others she would do. This time she had decided to say no.

And what was her reason for postponing the book? Oprah had decided it was more important now to have more time—more time for joy.

Success is also being able to delete what you have in mind. It's being able to eliminate an old habit, way of thinking, or way of reacting. Like completions, deletions release energy—energy you've had tied up and unavailable for years—so you can begin using it to create the experiences you want. So you can enjoy a healthy, balanced, fulfilling life.

Any skillful gardener knows, besides watering and fertilizing, a healthy plant needs regular pruning. Success is being able to let go of an unworkable method or system. An outgrown relationship you've tried everything conceivable to fix. A well-paying job you've done the same way far too many times. Success is quitting smoking or giving up caffeine, sugar, or drugs; or letting go of your society-rewarded addiction to old rules, hard work, money, or power. *Success is cutting out, down, or back.*

Each time we acknowledge that we have completed or deleted a creation cycle, a new quantum of energy is generated for our use. Each time we acknowledge ourselves as powerful, response-able creators, we become closer and closer to understanding that we are cocreating with God.

Highly Successful People Say Yes and No

observed over and over that highly successful people are able to say no. No, I don't want to do this. No, I can't take on another project now. No, it doesn't fit my priorities. No, it would unbalance my life. No. *Highly successful people are decisive; and decisive, like incisive, means able to cut away.* Able to *not* do, to *not* accomplish.

But if saying no is so important, then why is it so hard to say? Because *they* taught us no was an unacceptable answer. It led to upset and disapproval. It was cause for time-outs or privileges being taken away. It was the reason for a poor evaluation or being passed over for promotion. *Yes, somehow we were supposed to be able to say no to drugs but not to our parents or teachers or bosses or spouses or ministers or rabbis or priests.* But not being able to say no has led millions, or is it billions, of people to experience abuse—of themselves and others.

Success-Filing your deletions: Everything we do is done with a dream in mind. Is what I chose to do today because of a dream my dad had? Or my mother? Or my teacher? Or my boss? Or my spouse? Or my friend? And is this my dream, too, or simply a habit I might want to delete? Is what I chose to do today because of a dream my child had—my inner child or my own son or daughter? Is this my dream, too, or simply a habit I might want to delete? What did I decide *not* to do today? What did I decide was no longer worth investing time and energy in? What did I say no to? Who did I say no to? What old until-now unconscious ways of responding did I let go of?

It Took Months for Carly
to Turn Her Life Around

Within days the phone calls started again. Carly's office manager—now vice president—phoned to warn that her husband had just had another argument with a staff member and was on his way home. Next her husband called to let her know, in no uncertain terms, that he would be home in ten minutes and he expected her help. Even though she had known this test was coming, even though she had rehearsed how she would handle it—reminding him of her resignation and the vital reasons why—she still caved in, reassuming the savior role she had been playing for years. Once again her energy and vitality fell to almost nothing. And her doctor was concerned.

It took months of determination for Carly to begin turning her life around. The next time the new vice president called, Carly told her the problem was *hers*. The next time her husband said he was on his way home to be rescued, she said she was on her way to a yoga class *to save herself,* risking his rage being directed at her later.

Each time she stood her ground, he was forced to confront current reality. Unless she changed, she felt she would lose her life. Unless he changed, he would lose his staff, wife, and family—and he knew it. Like a tough-love friend, she pressed him to redefine success along with her.

Pain Is a Friend:
Responding to Alert Messages

It may sound strange but pain can be a friend—the kind who's willing to jump up and down and yell to alert you before disaster strikes. Reaching your goal from a bed in intensive care is the booby prize. Being remembered as "highly successful" posthumously is regrettable. Endlessly climbing higher and higher and never stopping to enjoy the view is pointless and unfulfilling.

To reach your dreams, you will need to program bottom-line *alert messages,* messages you pay attention to *no matter what.* Certain levels of pain in your stomach, back, or neck. A certain depth of depression that sends you out to seek help. Certain sensations of anxiety and confusion that make you find out what's happening. Alert messages include the shouts and warnings of family and friends who read the gauges on your control panel better than you do, who know you're traveling too fast or too slow. They whisper quiet hints at first. Then they speak louder and louder until they are shouting in your face: *You've got to do something before it's too late!*

He Gave Up His Family Instead of His Ideas About Success

When Greg's mother and brother walked into his condominium months later, he was gone, and he had left everything behind. The framed picture of him with his arm around his girlfriend still hung opposite the front door. Sheets, pillows, and comforters were still on the bed. Kitchen counters were stacked high with pizza boxes and chicken tubs. The refrigerator was running and full.

They wanted to know what happened. Why had he stepped out of his life like a crab shedding an unwanted shell and gone elsewhere? Why had he changed his name and refused to communicate with his family? His home was furnished in exquisite detail.

He had every high-tech gadget available. Greg appeared to be successful; he had money and power. But he didn't have something he desperately needed, something so important that he was willing to abandon his old life for the possibility of a new one.

Apparently Greg couldn't live with his unconscious ideas about success, and the only way he knew to survive was to start over in a new place with a new identity. But would he rise to the internal challenge of his choice? Would he be able to step away from the decisions he had made, the habits he had developed, the reactions he had stored in his mind and body? Yes, it looks like we can simply step free, but our parents' and society's thinking continues to run us. A mere change of external terrain does not change our internal terrain; it does not free us from our past. Or move us ahead to our desired future.

Greg held on to his definition of success and gave up his family. Carly held on to her family and redefined what she meant by success. She helped those around her to understand what she had in mind, to update their expectations and help balance their reactions. Greg was unwilling, or unable, to talk his upset through. Walking away might seem easier in the short term, but remember, whatever definition has you stuck will operate wherever you are, no matter whom you're with. You will have to keep leaving and leaving and restarting and restarting until you no longer blame others for your failure to find a definition of success that works.

Cutting and running doesn't solve the problem—it simply moves it farther on down the road. Yes, Greg's story is shocking but no more shocking than all the families that are left behind because of divorce. Why? Too long hours. Too many business calls at night. No time for our kids' ball games and assemblies. No time to communicate openly with the people who love us. Too committed to other outcomes *they* taught us we should complete to make family a priority.

Paying the Ultimate Price

George, the CEO of a major international business, grew up watching his father's frantic pace. His father was driven for good reason; he and his family escaped from Cuba and left everything behind. With absolutely nothing to fall back on, he had to make sure his business would survive.

But forty years later, George and his father were still managing their business the same way. For months George's mind, body, and coworkers had all been telling him to slow down. To delegate more. To take some time off. He had a short fuse and was constantly yelling, sweating and red-faced—putting in more hours than anyone could keep up with; calling meetings that started at 7:00 P.M.; traveling around the world to solve other people's problems without scheduling time to attend to his own exhaustion. He worked hard and played hard. Until one night around ten o'clock, when he told his wife that he wasn't feeling well and headed for the bathroom. A few minutes later, she found him dead on the floor. George was forty-two.

Where are you stuck in the success maze? Are you still looking for *their* acknowledgment? Do you still want *them* to manage your process step by step? Do you still want them to create your dreams for you? Or are you still trying to complete dreams they created in your mind years ago?

In ancient times, before you could enter the healing temple to be treated for whatever disease or discomfort you had, you were forced to make your way through an overwhelmingly complex giant maze. Archaeologists, who found these taller-than-a-man mazes and struggled through them, wondered why physicians would require diseased people to encounter so many barriers, turns, and obstacles before they could be healed.

The ancient sages tell us that to heal we must first allow ourselves to become disoriented—disoriented enough to let go of our old point of view and habitual approaches, the ways that made us diseased in the first place. We must be willing to move past, "Yeah, but . . . I know," "Leave me alone," or "My way is working" to "I don't know." We must allow ourselves to become disoriented in order to change. We are coming out on the other side of the maze as the creators of our lives, beginning to explore the skills *we* will need to begin leading *our* lives . . . skillfully.

What Is Failure?

Failure is simply incompletion, the inability to either complete or delete.

Actor Anthony Hopkins says no is his favorite word. "I've gone through most of my life saying yes when I should have said no." Only as he approached sixty did he realize what a powerful word no really is.

Failing to complete or delete robs us of the creative power we have but haven't owned. The truth is we are always creating what we have in mind. But once we recognize ourselves as creators, we can begin changing our minds and our realities.

People fail for different reasons. Sometimes they lack the skills to do what they have in mind, and they're unwilling to ask others to assist them. Sometimes they say yes to something they should have said no to. Sometimes they have conflicting ideas about what they have in mind that cancel each other.

Why is success confusing? Because we learned about success by example when we were children, and we didn't know the memories we were laying down in our brains day by day would determine what we wanted to complete in the future—what would propel us ahead unconsciously, and even unwillingly, at times.

Whose Idea About Success Are Keeping You Stuck?

Tom came to see me because he couldn't figure out what he wanted. He was a college graduate but hadn't been able to crank himself up to make good grades, good money, or anything else. Tom sensed something unconscious was blocking him. So together we began exploring what he had in mind about success—not just what people had told him but what he'd learned by example.

I asked Tom to name someone he thought was successful. Tom quickly responded, "My dad." After the army, his dad took a job as a longshoreman. For him, it was a great job—steady work and a steady paycheck. But Tom saw his dad's ideas about success fail. In the 1980s another port opened up nearby; Tom's dad kept his job, but his salary was cut in half! Why did Tom think his dad was successful? "Because my dad was a good provider. He worked hard and sacrificed a lot for his family." "So that's what success means to you?" I asked. "Well, yes, I guess it is," Tom replied. Using his dad's ideas about success as a reference point, Tom felt like a failure. He wasn't a good provider. He didn't have a steady job or kids of his own. He couldn't put down his head blindly and push like his dad. Even as a boy, Tom knew his father's ideas weren't right for him.

Tom didn't want to succeed his dad's way, but he didn't want to succeed his boss's way either. In five years Tom's boss had turned "an idea" into "a company" that he was selling for an astounding amount of money—plus a $100,000 consulting fee. But Tom's boss was also his friend, so Tom knew a side of him that nobody else knew. His boss was a stress eater—his weight had soared to more than three hundred pounds. And to relax, he liked to party. But after his arrest for drunk driving, Tom's boss became "more dependent than a sixteen-year-old without a license." Tom was the one who drove him to AA meetings. Tom was the one who handled his job while he was in jail and made excuses so that his boss's absence would appear "normal." Everybody else saw his boss as "successful," but Tom knew the cost.

Instead of succeeding in his father's or his boss's way, Tom thought he might be attempting to succeed in his mother's way—by just making it through each day (she had four boisterous boys) and trying to get some peace and quiet.

Our ideas about success come from many sources. But those sources don't always agree. Each of us is challenged to choose which parts to keep and to complete—and which parts to delete and to create newly.

Whose Agreement and Acknowledgment Are You Still Trying to Get?

Consciously or unconsciously, whom are you still trying to please? Whose dreams are you still trying to live out?

Etienne, a trash collector, was pruning a huge tree in my yard. He seemed so happy and centered that, with his permission, I began asking him questions about his life. He described his job, hours, and benefits, how much he loves working outdoors, and what he does in his time off. It all sounded wonderful. But as we continued talking I was surprised to hear him say he wasn't successful—he wasn't the lawyer his mother wanted him to be. With a caring chuckle, I asked Etienne if I could show him how his life looked through my eyes. And with a quick turn of his head toward me, he said yes.

"You have what seems like a perfect job for you. You are up in the morning early, the way you prefer. You work outside while it's cool and, if you and your team hustle, you are finished by noon. After that you're on your own with health benefits and retirement. Plus Mondays off. Afternoons and evenings, you are realizing your dream of teaching high-risk teenage boys—who would otherwise get in trouble—how to wrestle, how to exercise self-discipline, how to be coached and successful. You have a public-service TV wrestling show on Sunday afternoons, and you are starting a second wrestling school soon. Etienne, I know lots of highly educated, well-paid lawyers who would love to trade places with you!"

We are moving past old standards and criteria. Strikes and work stoppages have taught us the importance of what everyone does. How quickly a city grinds to a stop if its trash isn't picked up or its traffic isn't running freely, if it doesn't have electricity or clean and pure water. What are your passions, preferences, and talents? What are your dreams, and how can you begin making them come true?

It is time to stop judging ourselves by anybody else's standard and to begin creating our own lives—lives we know will make a contribution to the whole because each one of us has something we love to do, and be, that is needed.

Breakdown: But Would She Listen?

As long as the creation, management, and acknowledgment of our success belong to others, we remain trapped. Our minds, bodies, and spirits have been trying to tell us this truth our whole lives, alerting us in moments of disillusionment and breakdown to make the changes we want instead of numbing ourselves and abandoning our dreams. Listen to your body. It will tell you when you need to make changes.

Lillian had been a top sales producer in her industry for seventeen years. She was a master at attracting customers and serving them beyond their expectations. Even when her product prices were high, she could do business because of the relationships she consistently nurtured and grew.

But something had gone wrong in the last few years. Lillian just couldn't get herself on the phone anymore. She just couldn't get herself to follow up and through. She was no longer enthusiastic about her work or her life.

Her body had been trying to alert her that she had been doing the same thing the same way for too long; whenever she assumed her usual on-phone position, she felt tremendous neck pain. For several years she had been ignoring the accumulating signals, quitting one job after another, *blaming her outer situation instead of recognizing that she needed to work on the situation inside.*

Finally her mind and body took over, not letting her sleep for six days, pushing her harder and harder, faster and faster, accelerating her usual process until, exhausted, she ended up in the hospital. Unconsciously Lillian had created the perfect opportunity to delete what she was doing and choose again.

Would she use this breakdown to propel herself forward to what she wants to experience in her life? Or would the fact that her résumé is so perfect for getting a high-paying job in her industry suck her back in? Would her attachment to her current income and lifestyle keep her stuck? In Skill 2, you will hear about the new life Lillian created.

Are we so afraid of giving up what we've got that we are willing to stay stuck? Are we so afraid of confronting uncertainty that we won't take corrective actions?

3. Success Is Creation: Taking Over as the Creator of Your Life

The most joyous part of success is also the most challenging. To create what we want, we need to stop looking back to blame others. We need to get oriented and look ahead as creators.

Start *choosing* each moment of each day. Start testing your ideas. And let their consequences test you. Decide what you want to complete and delete, and if you don't like the consequences, be sure to rechoose. Instead of relying on unconscious habits and familiar methods, make new choices about everything.

What do I want to eat for breakfast, lunch, and dinner today? What kind of exercise would work best for my body now? Do I want to go to that noon meeting or have lunch with my friend? Do

I want to pick up this phone call or respond to a message later on? Do I have the time and energy to take on a new project, or should I tell its creator no? Do I want to go out to dinner tonight or stay home and rebalance? Do I want to plan something special to do with family or friends? Is there something new I want to start learning?

Success-Filing your creative successes: It is especially important to acknowledge and file your creative successes. These seemingly tiny minor decisions—consciously made—are actually profound choices that lead to the major changes that we want. What plans or projects did you create? What new methods or systems, such as a new way to store your clothes or organize your work, did you invent today? What realizations popped into your mind? What new directions seemed to call to you today?

For better or worse, we are the creators of our lives. How we react to events, not the events themselves, shapes our reality. At this point in my life, I am most grateful to my colleagues at the National Institute of Mental Health who laughed when I spoke up that fateful morning. Their response disoriented me and challenged me *to take the lead myself, to discover and explore on my own.* Perhaps if they'd agreed with me, we would have had an interesting conversation and nothing would have happened, at least in my life. I am grateful for my divorce, too. I was sure I would be married "till death do us part." I meant that vow sincerely when I was uttering it.

I remember how upset I felt when those disorienting events occurred and how eager I was for things to "get back to normal." But, like it or not, I was being pressed ahead. What did *I* want to do? Where did *I* want to live? What did *I* want to do at night and on the weekends? I even remember wanting someone to tell me. I was excited about the freedom but overwhelmed by the creative responsibility.

The Crucible of Creativity

I t gets boiling hot as we wade through our own resistance and uncertainty and discover what we want but don't know how to get. I remember those nights when my new idea woke me up and the rehearsals and conversations I had in my head. That was creativity brewing and percolating up from the depths.

As we move through the maze we have to expect, and include, confusion and ambiguity. We have to let the image of what we want fade in and out, to morph its shape unexpectedly, to be shattered by dissent until it coalesces newly.

Wanting certainty up front doesn't work. It forces us to make decisions before we are ready. It presses us to grab hold of "something" long before we have had time to create what we really want.

It takes pain and pressure to move us from *they won't let me* to *I don't know.* It takes strength and commitment to move from *I don't know* to *I'll figure out what and how.* It takes trust in ourselves and the creative process to move from *an idea* all the way to *a reality.*

After the initial struggle to hold on to their old life subsided, Michael and Karen began to recognize the gift the universe had masterfully laid in their hands. The value of their home had increased so much that by selling it they would have more than enough money to live someplace else far more easily—someplace that wants a small-town doctor with lots of big-city experience. A place where there are parents and children who can enjoy Karen's skills and generosity. Somewhere that has a house with acres of woods for them to walk their dogs. Someplace where they would finally have time together, time to remember why they fell in love in the first place. And so, with this in mind, Michael made a new proposal: Let us begin to consciously create a new life—the life we choose now. And Karen accepted.

Once we free ourselves from our old limits, we can begin searching for how to fulfill our unique mission knowing that *when everyone on our planet is fulfilling his or her mission, the mission of planet Earth will be fulfilled, too.*

The New Mother/New Manager Dilemma: Updating What You Success-File

One of my most cherished memories is of Marjorie, a slightly built, sixty-something woman in one of my early seminars. She had been sitting there quietly listening to people happily reiterating successes—using the usual definition of success. Then she raised her hand and stood up abruptly. With tears streaming down her face, she blurted out, "You've all had lots of successes but I've never been successful. I was never an A student, I've never had a job, never made money or won prizes or plaques or bonuses." Then she sobbed openly.

As I asked questions to discover more about her life, Marjorie told us she had raised six highly successful children—teachers, lawyers, writers, even an inventor—who were raising successful families. She happily listed their prizes and achievements. But she didn't see that they had any relevance to her. All her life she'd felt like a failure. In fact, that was the very reason she was here in the seminar: Her kids had sent her.

During the next several breaks I looked to see how Marjorie was doing, and I found her in the hall with people all around her, sharing and talking. On the last day of the seminar Marjorie raised her hand once again. This time she stood up proudly and elegantly: "I want to thank each and every one of you from the bottom of my heart. I came here a *failure*. But I leave here a *success*. My new thinking about success has changed my life forever."

New mothers and fathers are faced with a success crisis at the birth of their children. Suddenly, instead of enjoying the successes they're used to—getting up and exercising, taking a shower, heading to work, stopping to get the dry cleaning, going out in the evening—they are at a loss for *success as they know it*. Sleep-deprived, shower-deprived, independence-deprived, or out of work on maternity leave, they are hard-pressed to Success-File. After a few weeks, they feel down not just because of hormonal changes but because of success changes as well.

As parents we need to realize that our opportunities for success have expanded. What we can include in our Success File has suddenly begun to multiply. Not only can we file all the new things we are doing—preparing food, changing clothes and diapers, giving baths, smiling and cooing back, making our babies feel safe and acknowledged, making our child's needs a higher priority than our own—we can also file all the successes our children are having: the first time she grips our hand with those tiny, perfectly formed fingers; the first time he looks us straight in the eye and smiles knowingly; the first time she sits up or crawls or walks or rides a bike or sings or reads, or does any of those activities a little better; the first time he sleeps without a pacifier, rides without training wheels, or crosses a street without holding your hand.

As parents, our children's successes are our successes, too. Ultimately our greatest successes of all will be in supporting our children as they differentiate between our ideas about success, their society's ideas, and their own, and in living and modeling the skills they will need to lead their lives successfully.

Top producers experience a similar crisis when they step up into management. Suddenly the criterion for their success changes from *what they succeed in doing by themselves to what everyone they manage succeeds in doing.* Suddenly there is the opportunity to jump from *satisfaction,* which comes as a result of our own efforts, to *fulfillment*—"to realize all one's potentialities as a person" (*New Webster's Dictionary*)—which comes as the result of our leadership.

Make sure you file not only your own successes but the successes of those you lead at home, at school, at work, in your community, and in the world. We humans are like seeds that produce plants that produce seeds that produce hundreds and thousands and millions and billions of plants and seeds more.

How successful do you feel? That depends on you, on how you define success and on how willing you are to make time to Success-File. Success is not just aimed at or desired; success is feeling satisfied and fulfilled by what you choose to do and be on a daily basis. Now, with this new definition in mind, what successes can you add to those original fifteen to twenty? Make sure you file not just your completion successes but your deletion and creation successes as well—especially those that are uniquely your own, those other people might not recognize or agree with.

Feeling successful is an inner process each one of us needs to learn. To master this process, you need ten skills. Redefining success for yourself while learning to self-acknowledge is the first skill you need to begin leading *your* life . . . skillfully.

Success is completion.

Success is deletion.

Success is also creation and cocreation.

When your Success File is full, you feel success-full.

Success in your past gives you confidence in your future.

Shifting Your Approach

A s I focused in more closely on what highly successful people were doing, I began to recognize that, like a car, success has gears. These people were using more Success Gears than the rest of us, and the more efficiently they were using them, the more freedom, flexibility, and fulfillment they enjoyed— the more they were able to pass on what they'd discovered.

Success Has Three Gears

A s we drive, we use gears to move us ahead, slowly at first, then more quickly and easily. As we succeed, we use gears to move us ahead, too. *First Gear is for starting anything new. Second Gear is for accelerating into productivity and competition. Third gear is for breaking through into creativity and leadership.* No gear is better than any other; all are essential—each one has its own timing and use.

In today's world, most people are *unconsciously* limiting themselves to the First and Second Gears of Success. And the very gear designed for breaking through into the joy and fullness of our lives is rarely engaged. This is what is preventing us from leading *our* lives.

Let's take a quick look at the three Success Gears in action before we dig in to understand how each one should be used and *not* used. Learning to use the Internet is a good example. At first the idea is exciting. You know you'd like to do it, but you're not sure how, and considerations about time and computers start to come up. Taking a deep breath, you decide *I'm going to do it,* and you phone a friend who has been happily surfing for years. "Would you come over and walk me through it step by step?" With her standing there beside you, you start. "First you need to . . ." "But how do I . . . ?" "Here's how. . . . Yeah, that's better. . . . No, don't do that, do this instead. . . . Good, right, yeah, now you've got the hang of it."

First Gear is learning the basics. In First Gear, you depend on a leader to guide you step by step, whether in person, on the phone, or in writing, as you begin to use your new skill safely and correctly.

Then your friend goes home and you start practicing on your own. Because it may not seem as clear now as it did when she was there beside you, you call her to ask specific questions as you continue to build your new skill. Now instead of just trying to get on the Internet, you begin using it to find information and people. It's easier and faster now, except for occasional glitches that require an additional call or visit.

Second Gear is moving ahead to why you wanted to learn it in the first place—so you could use it. Confident and experienced, you pursue your goals and interests more efficiently. The next time you talk to your friend, you catch yourself sharing discoveries you've made and telling *her* how to use them.

Third Gear is breaking through what you've been taught—the

beginner set of rules and limits—to create your own way and pass on your discoveries. Now you take on your *own* student, stand beside him, teach him the basics, and get him up and running and creative. And then he teaches a friend. . . . This is how the Success and Leadership Process works—ideally.

But if you think back to learning how to drive, getting a degree, professional certification, license, or promotion, or building a new room on your home, the flow from gear to gear doesn't always go so smoothly. Let's see why.

The Pluses and Minuses of Automatic Transmissions

When I learned to drive, we were required to take the road test using a car with a manual transmission. First we had to learn what each gear was for and when to use it, in theory. Then we went out with our parents and practiced how to do it, lurching and stalling with a nervous father or mother beside us. When they thought we were ready, we'd head down to the Division of Motor Vehicles, and this time, with a state licensing inspector sitting beside us, we'd pass our test the first time, or several times later. Then, license in hand, we could begin driving on our own.

But there were so many accidents involving gears that more and more people began buying cars with automatic transmissions—transmissions designed to make sure *the right gear would be used at the right time, no matter who the driver was or how much skill he or she had.* Yes, this was an advantage to new learners and nervous parents, but it led to greater and greater inefficiencies later on. Because as race drivers, bike riders, and high- and low-speed machine makers will tell you, being able to choose the right gear at the right time makes accomplishing whatever you have in mind far easier.

Millennia ago, society also designed an "automatic transmission" to make sure our success potential would be protected from serious accident or fatal injury. Until we're old enough or skillful enough, our parents, teachers, and employers are responsible for shifting our Success Gears for us. Age-appropriate, standardized, government-regulated, career-tracked—now our natural shifting points are frequently delayed or prevented *not because we're not ready but because someone else isn't.*

A college student recently discovered a passion for golf so he decided to drop out of school for a year to decide what part he might want that sport to play in his future. But when he shared his plan with his dad, he quickly reacted, "That's a bad idea, son. Stay in college."

Satisfied he'd offered good advice, the father told a friend what he'd said. And his friend replied tongue in cheek, "That advice is great if you want your son to have a reason to blame you for the rest of his life!"

A bit shaken, the father went back to his son. This time he suggested he call the counseling center at his university, fully expecting them to come down solidly on his stay-in-school side. But the University of Pennsylvania said they regularly encourage students to take time off to pursue dreams. And, since he was an excellent student, they would welcome him back after one year or even several.

Why was this father upset? He was upset because—*according to his standards*—his son was shifting gears too soon. *He was no longer depending on his father to shift for him; he was beginning to shift according to his own standards and dreams.*

If your car's automatic transmission wasn't working, you would quickly realize that your car wasn't accelerating to cruising speed or slowing down smoothly and take it in for repairs instead of attempting to drive to work or pick up your kids. *But the "automatic transmission" in our lives is not working*—not allowing us to shift up into creativity and dream building, or down into health and relaxation. And people either don't realize it or don't know what to do about it. In our busy lives, we don't have the time and energy to continue doing what doesn't work. Let's stop now to take a closer look at what each Success Gear is used for, when to use it, and what happens when Success Gears are used incorrectly. Then, with this overview in mind, you will be prepared to recognize and use each gear and know when you're shifting too soon or too late.

Shifting into First Gear: Following a Leader

The First Gear of Success is for starting a new life, skill, school, job, or relationship—or for starting over when what you're doing isn't working and you aren't getting the results you want. To shift into First Gear you must overcome the inertia of old fears and inabilities and start moving from "thinking about" to doing. This is a tall order and we'll spend a great deal of time looking at it in detail later on.

How do you know you're successful in First Gear? Whatever you're learning—accounting, law, sales, or teaching—you know you're successful when your leader tells you; that is, when he or she acknowledges that you are performing your new skill effectively, *according to his or her standards and rules.*

Ideally in First Gear you have a leader beside you—at home, in school, or in a corporate setting—but sometimes you have to lead yourself through First Gear, picking up a manual and following it step by step or finding your way hit or miss. Whether you are learning to install a new car seat or to operate a VCR, you need to learn the basics before you can proceed productively. To succeed in First Gear, you must be willing and able to follow your leader's instructions precisely.

That may have been easy for you as a kid, but it's much harder for you as an adult because you're used to being independent, productive, and competitive. And because you have memories of leaders who failed you. Shifting into First Gear limits your freedom and makes you dependent. But, like training wheels, learner's permits, and apprenticeships, *that limit only needs to remain in place until you've developed enough information and experience to proceed on your own.* Just as your car's first gear was never designed to get you all the way to work or your favorite resort, the First Gear of Success was never designed to get you all the way to the destinations you dream of. It's for starting.

While your leader is teaching you how to perform your new skill, he or she also needs to be modeling how to Success-File your new skill, taking time to acknowledge what you're accomplishing—all the tiny parts you're doing better now than five minutes ago, yesterday, or last week. Then, as you begin to recognize your own successes, your leader needs to start handing over the Success-Filing responsibility to you; he or she should *ask* you what successes you've had instead of *tell* you, then listen attentively to ones you list and add ones you failed to notice or thought unworthy of mention. *Your First-Gear leader is responsible for making sure your Success File is full every day, helping you build the confidence you need to continue succeeding.*

First-Gear items to add to your Success File: Here are some basics we need to complete to lead our own lives successfully. We are safe, healthy, and rested. Our bodies are clothed, well fed, and exercised. The cars we drive are in good repair and fueled. Our homes, tech equipment, and appliances are working. Our bills are paid. We acquire the new skills we need. We rest, relax, and have fun. We take care of the people and relationships that make our lives joyful.

Ideally in life we learn one thing at a time, but from time to time we find ourselves in the First Gear of *almost everything.* This was how it was a lot when we were kids, but for adults this circumstance usually occurs because of a death or divorce, when we marry, or when we change jobs, cities, homes, friends, and towns.

The Vocabulary of First Gear

The following words signal when you or someone else is in the First Gear of Success: excited, eager, anxious, scared, feeling unsafe, trusting/distrusting, follow, try, question, safe, rules, limits, good/bad, right/wrong, can/can't, should/shouldn't, morality, integrity, have to, must, always/never, possible/impossible, certain/uncertain, control, praise, correction, supervision, effective, competent, consistent, test, permit, allow, overly dependent and fearful, needing constant input, rule-driven, unbending, rigid, bureaucratic, limited, angry, resentful. These words give you a feel for what is *most desirable—and most destructive—*about First Gear, *depending on how you use it.*

In these moments we need to recognize that we aren't having a nervous breakdown; we're simply overwhelmed because we are operating in First Gear in so many areas at once. At these times, we need to reach out for support and leadership to friends and family who know us, or professionals who can guide us.

When should you shift into Second Gear? When you are performing your new skill safely, effectively, and consistently. As an adult you may be able to decide on your own when you're ready, but when you were a child or a student or new in your job that decision usually wasn't yours to make. It was up to your leader—your "automatic transmission."

Shifting into Second Gear: More-Better-Faster

In Second Gear our productivity accelerates. Certified, licensed, or authorized, we begin practicing our new skill. The training session is over and we're back at our desks with goals and projections already set up for us. Now, with quantity and quality pressure and no leader beside us, we begin deciding which start-up rules and steps we still need to use and which ones we can delete. In Second Gear, shortcuts become a must; they will make the difference between winning and losing, moving ahead and falling behind. But these shortcuts must work, and some of them won't.

How do you know you're successful in Second Gear? Your results will tell you. Your scores, grades, charts, and graphs show when your performance is up or when it's sliding. In Second Gear you need to continue increasing your productivity to keep measuring up, to become competitive and get promoted. *But who determines those grades, promotions, positions, and increases?* Who creates those charts, graphs, and projections? *They do*—your parents, teachers, bosses, and society. Even though you seem to be a highly independent professional, *you are still dependent on other people to make you feel successful.*

Now instead of waiting for that immediate *good or bad, right or wrong*, you are waiting around for days, weeks, or even months for those charts to go up or those promotions, perks, and bonuses to be announced—the input you need to gauge whether you're successful or not. You trust yourself as long as your results are going up. But when there's a drop and your confidence plummets, you head off in search of leaders for input and detail. After all, it's *their* dream you are working to complete.

Just as second gear in your car wasn't designed to get you to work or your workout, the Second Gear of Success wasn't designed to get you to your dream—it was designed to get you to the dreams of others who pay you so that you have the resources to produce dreams of your own. Once you've mastered creating *their* dreams, you can apply what you've learned to create *your own.*

Second-Gear items to add to your Success File: To lead our lives, we need to make sure we're completing our Second-Gear needs. We have an area of our lives in which we're productive, raising kids or making our companies the best in the field. We produce results

The Vocabulary of Second Gear

The following words signal when you or someone else is in the Second Gear of Success: produce, compete, more-better-faster, win, lose, scores, grades, appraisals, evaluations, pressure, short-cuts, rewards, losses, money, higher, lower, charts, graphs, quotas, quantity vs. quality, struggle, marketing, promotions, investment accounts, credit card balances, interest, campaigns, strategies, bonuses, position, title, wealth, power, retirement accounts, stock prices, buyouts, takeovers, stress, vacation getaways, workouts, weight gains and losses, caffeine, ulcers, checkups, tranquilizers, high blood pressure, exhaustion, politics, spinning, cheating, anger, debt, depression, drugs, collapse. These words give you a feel for what is *most desirable—and most destructive*—about Second Gear, *depending on how you use it.*

on time at the level expected or even better. We hire people to do some things we no longer have time to do, providing more money for them and more time for us. We hire lawn cutters, house-keepers, painters, and plumbers. We pay for baby-sitters and day care. We join car pools. We pay for pickup and delivery. We eat out more, work out more, and get more massages, chiropractic treat-ments, and acupuncture. We do whatever it takes to manage our lives in new and improved ways. And in the process we learn to manage and acknowledge ourselves and others.

Ideally in life we use all three gears each day. But from time to time we may find ourselves in the Second Gear of *almost everything*, pressed against deadlines and client demands and racing to keep up. In these moments we need to take a few minutes, hours, or days to take stock. When is enough enough? How many clothes, cars, toys do we really need? And what are all those possessions costing us—not just in money but in time, space, and energy we could use in ways more aligned with our dreams?

Most people Success-File money, titles, and promotions, but make sure you also include timely shortcuts, day-to-day improvements, and powerful corrections, as well as Second-Gear excesses you are deleting.

Where Is the Shifting Point Between Second and Third Gears?

The beginning of the Second Gear of our careers is exciting. Whew! We've made it through school and training and we're gainfully employed, so we begin rewarding ourselves, buying and owning things *they* taught us to dream about having—cars, homes, nice furniture, and expensive clothes. And we start doing things *they* taught us we should do—getting married, having kids, working toward promotions, perks, and bonuses—those fifteen to twenty successes most people write down. Occasionally we have a setback and need to gear down into First again to learn a new skill or make a correction; however, things in general are good. But given increasing costs and expenses, the new baby, mortgage payments, and credit card balances we've added, we start feeling the pressure of our Second-Gear Success—the pressure to do more-better-faster.

No, there is nothing inherently wrong with Second Gear; in fact, it's essential. It's what makes us productive and allows us to pay our bills and build our families and businesses. It's what makes our world work—better transportation, utility, communication, financial, and security systems, better education, health care, and retirement systems. There's nothing wrong with the Second Gear of Success any more than there is something wrong with the second gear of your car. What's wrong is your "automatic transmission"—the pervasive pressure to stay in Second Gear too long.

Whether we realize it or not, we live in a Second-Gear society, one committed to productivity and competition, money and power. That's what is advertised and promoted as "success." That's what is disproportionately rewarded and bonused and perked. That's why we're working so long and so hard. That's why we've gotten so far away from First-Gear needs and values. That's what those middle-school kids thought "success" is and why they were resisting it. But success has three essential gears.

Some people catch on to the credit card game and cut back on spending. They take time to rethink their dreams and decide for themselves which ones they want to pursue. But many people get caught up in the adrenaline rush of so much activity and material success that they don't see what is happening to their health and their families. They don't see the cost until a crisis occurs, or they ignore numerous crises. Then, like Carly, they start asking themselves, *But when is enough enough?*

The shift from First to Second Gear was decided for us. So perhaps there is an unconscious assumption that the shift from Second to Third Gear will be decided for us as well. But it won't. This is a shift you must make for yourself. But when?

The Third Gear of Success: You Must Shift into It "Manually"

More-better-faster and more-better-faster still until it finally becomes perfectly clear that the method you've spent all this time honing is no longer producing results. And one morning you wake up thinking *Aha! There's another way I can do this. I just thought of a new system, product, or service, a better way to live my life. And I feel compelled to share it.*

Most inventors report that they weren't sitting at their desks when their creative ideas hit them; they were taking a shower or walking in the woods or working on something else altogether. They weren't pressing harder and harder, but they had eased up on the gas the way you do in a manual-transmission car when you shift up into third gear.

The shift to Third Gear isn't something that can be mandated or legislated or done for you. It is a shift you must know is possible and make for yourself. But most people don't believe that it's possible. The First-Gear rule-followers don't. The Second-Gear results-followers don't. So they continue doing things the same way, even though they aren't living the lives they want. Despite breakdown after breakdown, crisis after crisis, they don't shift. Why?

Sometimes the reason is because the rules of First Gear were written with permanent markers—word markers that indicate they are permanent, unchangeable, un-updateable. Words like *always/ never, can/can't, have to/must, possible/impossible* are limits that the obedient can never reexamine or change. So these people live behind First-Gear success limits their whole lives, or until someone teaches them when and how to shift into Second Gear.

Sometimes people don't shift into Third Gear because the rewards of Second Gear are financially skewed toward pressing harder and harder using existing methods; the systems are already up and running and paid for, even though they are no longer working efficiently, no longer competitive, no longer producing the desired result.

But most often people don't shift because they are unaware of the Success Gears and how vital it is to shift up and down as needed.

You Will Need a Well-Constructed Dream to Shift into Third Gear

So how do you shift into Third? Not by jettisoning your whole life. When you feel burned out and run ragged, the thought of quitting your job, selling your home, and leaving your marriage may be tempting. But throwing it all away won't move you ahead. The shift to Third Gear must be smooth and gradual, or you'll find yourself stalled in First Gear again.

In Third Gear, instead of "follow the leader" you "follow your dream," allowing it to guide you all the way to completion and enjoyment. To shift into Third Gear, you will need to start dreaming again—the way you used to dream as a kid, sketching at first, then adding more and more appealing details and colors.

In Third Gear you must be more committed to your dream than to past limits and leaders, leading yourself ahead instead of blaming those you feel may have led you astray. Your various leaders knew what they wanted *for you,* and in First and Second Gears that was appropriate and even helpful. But to shift into Third, you will need to discover what *you* want for yourself. You will need to begin asking yourself day by day, moment by moment, *What do I want? And what is wanted of me? Why am I here?*

But before you can shift, you will need to take your foot off the gas. Maybe that means getting away for a few days or even weeks, and investing that precious time in paying attention to what you've been going too fast to notice. I'm talking about the simplest things: eating right, relaxing, napping when you're tired, spending time with friends and family, getting enough sleep. Use this time to make contact with your body again; when you wake up, sense how tired you feel before you drink a quick cup of coffee or go for a run to pump yourself up. Use it to wean yourself off Second-Gear habits. Use it to refocus on *your* life.

Sculpting the Life You Want

In Third Gear you'll be like Michelangelo standing before a virgin block of marble, asking yourself, *What will I cut away?*

You can't shift into Third and keep doing everything you've been doing, but that doesn't mean you'll have to give up what's important. It does mean that you'll have to start *passing* on parts of it. If beautiful dinners are important, you can order in delicious, colorful food, set the table, and light candles. If spending more time with family is important, you can re-create your job or teach others to do parts of it and begin leading. And, if some things are no longer essential, you can decide *not* to do them at all. You can delete them.

The truth is, you have shifted into Third Gear many times in your life—every time you had one of those middle-of-the-night, electric-charge-passing-through-your-body *Aha!*s But for most people those ideas remained simply that—ideas to be stored in their "Someday I'll File." As attractive as their ideas seemed at the moment, they soon forgot about them or kept them secret and used them to hone their own competitive edge, immediately shifting back into Second Gear. But after you break down over and over and gear up from First into Second and hit the same wall again and again, *there comes a moment when you choose to break through: I want my life to be different. And this time I will do it!*

Third Gear is about identifying and realizing your vision for yourself, your business, your community, and, by extension, your world. In Third Gear the inner-knower—the part of you that knows you know—finally emerges; your inner-knower is connected to something much larger, something universal, a force or energy some call God. Suddenly you are no longer isolated and alone but a part of the whole—a part with something unique to contribute, a part that is no longer self-serving but eager to serve others with the knowledge that each of us is here on a mission. And your mission, when you discover it, will bring you fulfillment.

When we reach Third Gear, we finally integrate success and spirituality. In Third Gear we realize we're creators, too.

What Is Success?

Let's revisit the question we started exploring in Skill 1. What is success? At this point, we need to redefine success once again. *Success has different meanings depending on which Success Gear you're in:*

The Vocabulary of Third Gear

The following words signal when you or someone else is in the Third Gear of Success: Aha!, insight, realization, dream, create, plan, intend, manage, communicate, codream, cocreate, sharing the details, team building, open, listening, flexible, responsive, re-create, respecting new ideas, patient, including, cooperating, trusting, intuition, coincidence, synchronicity, knowing, whole, holographic, magic, guidance, inner-knower, prayer, guidance, cocreating with a Higher Force, too far out there, a space head, living in a dream world, a hopeless dreamer, full of harebrained schemes but can't pay his or her bills. These words give you a feel for what is *most desirable—and most destructive—* about Third Gear, *depending on how you use it.*

Success in First Gear is following rules and earning praise.

Success in Second Gear is producing results and getting ahead.

Success in Third Gear is creating your dreams, alone and with others.

To lead your life skillfully you will need to manually shift up and down as circumstances and conditions require, just as a skillful driver does.

Finding New Balance

Remember Lillian, the master saleswoman whose breakdown you read about in Skill 1? Well, a week after she was released from the hospital, her company fired her. Yes, just like that. But in retrospect it was perfect timing—time to escape the Success Trap. Lillian began using the rest of the Success Skills you will be learning in Part 2. She started creating powerful dreams (or holograms); when she shared them with others, they wanted to help her by providing information and connections. These dreams were so powerful that fears from her past couldn't scare her back into doing what she'd been doing before and so dear to her heart that she would be able to hold on to her outcome and explore methods until she found ones that worked for her.

Lillian realized, in retrospect, that she had devoted more time and energy to creating her career than her life. One of the dreams she'd shelved years ago was to find someone to love with whom she could create a marriage and a home. Because she had been hurt several times, this dream had been easy to shelve! But she dusted it off and, renewed, she began dating and choosing and rechoosing until she found a man she really wanted to get to know—moving slowly was something she wanted to do *this* time. But meanwhile she did something outrageous. She bought a puppy! What a delight her little white Fuzzy was, and what a creator of disasters. But Lillian could feel him changing her life. His love was warming her heart. His loyalty was offsetting old pain. And she was laughing and playing even when she caught herself saying *I'm too busy.* Such good preparation for a relationship, she told herself.

Lillian learned how to shield her new dreams not just from *her* doubts and fears but from the doubts and fears of other people, especially her protective mother. She practiced switching all the reasons *why not* that kept cropping up into restatements of *what she did want instead.* In shaky moments, she remembered the successes she'd created and Success-Filed and took time to relive them so she could keep going. Only too aware of what happened when she worked too long and too hard, when she skipped meals and was too revved up to sleep, she committed to maintaining her balance *no matter what.* She started paying attention to signals she now realized meant she was off. Eating and exercising became number one priorities, items she wrote on her schedule so she'd be sure to have time for them. No excuses would work anymore!

One of the first dreams Lillian chose to create was a way to share the love and wisdom her little puppy Fuzzy was giving her. Lillian wanted to share how much a loving animal can contribute. So she got Fuzzy licensed! Yes, trained and certified for pet therapy. Now they regularly go to hospitals and nursing homes together, while Lillian continues the process of creating other parts of her life.

And most profound of all, Lillian knows that if the next thing she commits to doesn't work out, she will have all the Success Skills she needs to figure out what comes after that.

Life is a process of creating, acknowledging, and deleting—and recreating, acknowledging, and deleting as we learn more and more about ourselves and others.

We Started Our Lives in Third Gear

Two-year-old Sam stood watching a painter apply a new color to his parents' bedroom wall. He wanted to paint, too, so he asked the painter if he could. To get Sam to abandon his outcome (and to leave the bedroom), the painter said Sam couldn't paint because he didn't have a paintbrush. But Sam knew what he wanted and was determined to get it. Like most children, he was operating in Third-Gear creativity and can-do. So Sam headed out on a mission. "That's not the end of this," his mom chuckled. "You wait and see." As predicted, a few minutes later Sam returned with a smile on his face. "Look," he proclaimed, brandishing his hairbrush. "I'm ready to paint with you."

If I can't do it one way, I'll do it another—that's the spirit we were born with. Or as my grandmother used to say, *Where there's a will there's a way.* But, as we saw in Skill 1, we soon learn that to succeed with parents, teachers, and society we needed to be able to use two other Success Gears: First, we needed to learn how to be effective and safe. Second, we needed to become efficient and productive. And now, all these years later, we are finally remembering what we already knew as kids: *A joyful life is about dreams, ours and others we choose to align with.*

In First and Second Gears other people created your dreams for you, but to shift into Third you must learn to construct dreams for yourself, not sketchy little "Someday I'll" dreams, but detailed, scientifically well-constructed dreams *you and your team* can carry all the way to completion. That's what you'll learn to do in Skill 3.

Most of the dreams we have as busy adults are ones that require us to become powerful leaders—leaders who are so clear about what we want that we can stay on course even when we are bombarded by friendly opinions or expert advice. Remember, if you lose confidence in yourself (keep on Success-Filing) and your dream, you will probably shift back into First or Second Gear and head in *their* direction instead. *And yes, they will be thrilled with your results, but you won't be.*

Before you begin managing a project—investing time, energy, and money; hiring carpenters, painters, architects, contractors, advisers, consultants, or employees—let's take a closer look at leaders, not at government or corporate heads but at *you* as a leader, the leader of *your* life.

Three Mirrorlike Leadership Gears: Which Gear Do They Need Me to Be In?

As a leader, you will need to be able to shift Success Gears up and down to meet not only your needs but also the needs of people you're working with.

The First Gear of Leadership is leading new learners to success.

The Second Gear of Leadership is leading producers to success.

The Third Gear of Leadership is cocreating with creators.

As a leader, you will need to look *not just from your perspective but also from the perspective of the person you are leading*. Take a minute to determine which Success Gear the person you're working with is in. Then ask yourself: Which Leadership Gear do *I* need to shift into now to support him or her? Is this person new at what I'm asking him to do? Or is she already schooled, licensed, and professional in this area? Is this person in Second Gear or operating in Third, already generating ideas about how to meet my needs and complete my dream? Your ability to answer these questions—before taking action—will determine your success or failure as a leader.

Shifting up and down skillfully will allow those you are leading to succeed whether they are learning the basics, accelerating their productivity, or breaking through old limits into creativity and innovation. In First Gear they need constant supervision and guidance. In Second Gear they still need you nearby—in person, by phone, or by E-mail—to help them make decisions and provide feedback and correction. They need you to evaluate their results on a regular basis so that they won't veer too far off course without correction. And no matter which Success Gear they are in, they will need you to Success-File with them on a regular basis.

The Third Gear of Leadership is a shift many leaders fail to make, because they are more familiar with followers and competitors than creators, more comfortable telling and managing than cocreating. To cocreate you will need to not only construct your dream holographically (you will learn this technique in Skill 3) but communicate your dream holographically as well (Skill 4) so that you can inspire, involve, and draw forth others' creativity and enthusiasm. They can then give you new ideas.

Success-Filing all of the Success and Leadership Gears: Now that you understand Success Gears, it's time to add some more successes to your file. What First-Gear successes did you have today (successes achieved by following a leader's start-up rules and directions, taking baby steps to something new, overcoming fears and trying new behaviors)? What Second-Gear successes did you produce today? What did you do more quickly and easily than before? What did you do that exceeded goals and expectations? What prizes did you win, what acknowledgments did you receive? What raises, promotions, or bonuses did you earn? What Third-Gear successes did you enjoy today? What new ideas, methods, goals, or dreams did you create? What did you realize or discover?

And what successes did you lead others to today, in First, Second, and Third Gears? In what ways were you a more skillful leader than before?

Shifting Errors

So now that you understand all three Success Gears and all three Leadership Gears in theory, shifting gears should be easy. But here's the rub: You have memories.

Because your leaders probably didn't know about all gears and their parents didn't either, the behaviors you have recorded in memory may be quite different from the skills you've been reading about. Remember, whenever you are in new situations your brain automatically and unconsciously accesses past memories—how you felt when you dented your dad's car and he yelled; how embarrassed you felt when your teacher humiliated you for asking too many questions, or too few; how upset you were when your boss complained that you weren't learning fast enough—to decide what to do in the moment. And so even though you know better now, you may catch yourself replicating memorized behaviors and re-creating your leadership past instead of creating the future you want, unless you stay alert.

As you read the stories of Barbara and Tom, think about how the Success and Leadership Gears apply to their situations, and what you would do instead . . . knowing what you know now.

Her Leaders Didn't Recognize Her Gear-Shifting Ability . . . Until It Was Too Late

Barbara was the sales manager of a major museum. A graduate of one of the country's best universities, she had a résumé anyone would envy and enough energy to do whatever she had in mind. But no one had ever taught her about shifting gears.

Barbara was accelerating along in Second Gear, multiplying the museum's sales by 1,100 percent, bringing in huge corporate clients, socializing in her off-hours with people who could bring in even more business—generating the results a typical American corporation would be thrilled with, plus dreaming up new ways for making the museum more money. But Barbara didn't understand that she was working for people who were operating in First Gear. So instead of acknowledging the results she was producing, they criticized her for being one minute late to meetings or how loud her heels clicked along the marble hallways.

Barbara's confidence plummeted and she couldn't figure out why. She kept looking at *her results* instead of recognizing what her First-Gear employers had in mind. They were into right and wrong, have-tos and musts, *not* her performance. Once she understood that they were stuck in First Gear, she resigned. A year later they were still interviewing, unable to replace Barbara—and her results—with someone who would operate in First Gear along with them.

Barbara is a painter and photographer, and the reason she chose to work for the museum in the first place was to learn how to market her own art. In touch with her dream again and acknowledging what she'd learned, she decided the universe was sending her a message: It was time to gear down to make a change. So she started Success-Filing every day to rebuild the confidence and enthusiasm she would need. This time, when she was cranking in Second Gear, her art sales would serve as a gauge for how well she was doing. This time her customers would appreciate her creative new ideas.

Barbara understands that to get there she needs to concentrate on Success-Filing more than on how much money she makes: She needs to Success-File her whole life—how carefully she is eating and exercising; how much she is enjoying friends and family; how much she is learning and improving; how creative she is (the wonderful photographs she took of the blazing morning sky in Key West); how healthy and whole everyone says she seems these days. And how happy she feels as she stands covered in bright splotches of paint surveying her new studio and the huge conference room next door, both filled with vibrant new canvases. Barbara is back on track to her dreams. Understanding Success Gears allowed her to move forward consciously instead of unconsciously remaining stuck in a job that didn't fit.

Not Doing Unto Others What Was Done Unto You: Creating a New Vision for Leaders

As Tom and I continued exploring why he didn't know what he wanted to do with his life, why he couldn't get clear about his dreams and direction, an old memory came up, one that had haunted him every time he thought about going back to school to redirect his career or learn anything else.

Tom told me about a scary feeling he'd had whenever he was around a particular priest who taught him in elementary school. The priest used to make Tom sit on his lap in front of the class. He told Tom he was his favorite. But Tom was afraid of him and he wasn't sure why. Finally Tom ran home sobbing and told his mom he thought that priest wanted to hurt him. And she responded, "You must be mistaken, Tom. He's such a nice man." But he wasn't. Several years later the priest was arrested for sexually assaulting a student in that school. Tom had been right to be afraid of that particular teacher but not every teacher for the rest of his life!

Just as Tom was leaving my office, I received an urgent call from a young mother who was distraught about a situation involving her two-and-a-half-year-old son. That morning, when Emily dropped Eric off at day care, another parent asked if she'd heard that a teacher there had been accused of tying a "bad" student to a chair and taping his mouth shut. Emily hadn't heard that, but she immediately set about checking and, after numerous calls, found out the rumor was true.

Now, four hours later, Emily was calling to tell me that she had already enrolled her son in another school and let the other parents know what was being covered up. She wanted to know who else she should inform so that immediate changes could be made to insure the safety of the other children. *If it could happen to any child in that school, it could happen to my son,* she reasoned. And that was not a chance she was willing to take.

When Tom overheard what Emily had done, he began sobbing. "Oh God, I wish my mother had done that for me!"

Now *we* are society, each one of us. And our First-Gear responsibility is to assure that when someone is in the First Gear of success, he or she is safe anywhere in the world. We cannot learn unless we are able to let go of our safety and entrust it to our leaders. That is society's loftiest responsibility.

And *we*, as society, must simultaneously assure that when someone is striving to be productive and competitive we will lead him or her skillfully. When someone has a brilliant idea, he or she will be listened to and supported. Business owners and leaders must be prepared to meet the needs of individuals in all three gears.

What are the problems that face us as a planet? What safeties and securities do we need to constantly monitor and assure? What support to productivity do we need to implement and oversee? What support to creativity, new discoveries, methods, and systems do we need to provide to help us move beyond competitive barriers? What ideas that currently seem impossible may be possible soon?

Dream Your Children's Dreams with Them:
All She Wanted Was to Go Up in Space

As we begin using all three Gears of Success and Leadership, children become a source of inspiration. They are already in Third Gear, even though First and Second Gears are not yet in place. They haven't forgotten how to dream; they haven't already had their dreams knocked out of them. So it is one of our most sacred responsibilities to dream their dreams with them. What will they be when they grow up? And how can *we* help them?

Before my last talk at the middle school where I was invited to teach *The Technology of Success,* I mingled in the hallway introducing myself to participants. I would soon be speaking to this room full of eager parents about Success and Leadership Gears and, as the crowd pressed in on me, I found myself face-to-face with a smiling, well-dressed woman with a sparkle in her eye. She told me a story she hoped I would share.

When her daughter was five, she was fascinated with the NASA astronauts. Every time there was a space shot, she lay sprawled on the floor in front of the TV, eyes glued for hours. She talked endlessly about someday—that sacred time in the future—when she, too, would be an astronaut and go up in space.

The woman and her husband didn't take their daughter's dream seriously at first, chuckling to themselves at the very image of her strapped in a space capsule. But the girl could clearly see that scene playing out in her mind. She could imagine herself climbing on board in her space suit, well prepared for weightlessness. After a year, her dream had not faded. In fact it had become even more clear and detailed. And she was ready to take action. "Is there a camp where I can go to become an astronaut? Would you call NASA and ask?" *In that moment the woman and her husband finally got it. Their daughter's dream could come true, if she was prepared.* So they made that call to NASA and learned about a camp that would begin training her for precisely that career.

That day the girl's parents changed direction 180 degrees, from chuckling and dismissing their daughter's dream as *impossible*, to talking with her teachers, helping with science projects and contests, always being there to cheer her on when she won. Or didn't. They shifted into whichever Leadership Gear she needed them to be in at the time, depending on whether she was afraid, competitive, or simply going for it.

And you will be happy to know that their daughter was a crew member on a NASA space mission. She really was strapped in. She really was well prepared for weightlessness. As the rocket roared off the launching pad, shaking the ground below them, her parents stood arm in arm, in tears, celebrating their ability to hold their daughter's dream with her, to shift gears up and down with her, and even to live that dream with her.

The three Leadership Gears are mirrorlike reflections of the three Success Gears—the other side of where you were in each one. This is your opportunity to give someone else the kind of leadership you deserved but may not have received. What will it take to move beyond what they didn't tell you? It will take a well-constructed dream. A dream so attractive it will magnetize you to it. A dream so powerful even your worst experiences can't pull you backward. A dream your brain can begin using as a reference point. Where am I going? I'm heading for my dreams now.

Let's dig in and get started.

Part Two

The Rest of the Skills You Will Need

TO MAKE
THE CHANGES
YOU WANT

The Science of
Dreaming

Your ability to create dreams opens the gate to Third Gear. Third Gear is profoundly different from First and Second Gears. This path is not clearly laid down and marked like a well-traveled highway. This is the path of the explorer, who is constantly tuned in, searching for clues, noticing, sensing.

In Third Gear you must trust yourself and your unfolding process. Knowing how to Success-File (Skill 1) and how to operate in all three gears (Skill 2) will provide the foundation. Memories of past successes will provide the confidence you will need. If you were able to succeed then, you can succeed now.

In Third Gear, you are creating and following a dream, or a hologram, wherever it leads you. Like a painter, you begin with a sketch, a vague, hazy, undetailed thought, and little by little, day by day *add* more detail—more lines and crosshatches, more layers of color and pattern, more sound and dialogue, more emotion and energy. With a detailed dream clearly in mind, you begin to attract experiences that lead you to your dream. According to highly successful people, these experiences usually occur *when you are relaxing or thinking about something else altogether.*

Stepping into the Window of Your Dream

When Academy Award–winning actress Geena Davis started her acting career, she also worked in a department store. For some time she had been thinking about how she could become better known and decided being a model might be a way she could try. One day at work, she noticed a group of mannequins enjoying lunch together in the store window. There was one seat left at the table. To explore what modeling would be like, she climbed into the window and sat there with the mannequins.

A huge crowd gathered outside on the sidewalk, peering and pointing with curiosity and delight. Then her boss saw her: *"Get out of that window this minute or . . . I'll fire you!"* But when he caught sight of the crowd of potential customers outside the window, he changed his mind: "No! Stay right there and do what you're doing." And he hired her to model in that window on weekends.

Instead of watching our dreams from the outside, we must step into them to become successful. That's what we did as children and that's what we need to learn to do again as adults. But since those early, excited days, we have learned to delay and disconnect instead of following our instincts.

We Began Our Lives Dreaming

I loved the scream of the freight train as it rattled through our neighborhood each morning before dawn. Over and over at breakfast I chanted, "I want to ride on that train. I want to pull that whistle." Then one Saturday my dad took me on that train ride. We lurched back and forth, balancing and rebalancing our bodies all the way to the front of the train—passing through those noisy spaces between cars, opening and closing those heavy doors—so I could meet the engineer and pull that screaming whistle for myself.

Our childhood years were exciting, detailed, and powerful. We would lie in bed with our eagerly anticipated next day's experiences racing through our minds and bodies until it was finally time to get up. We were so unaffected by obstacles that our parents called us pests. "But Dad, the train will still run if it rains. But Mom, it will be fun getting up when it's dark. Oh no, Dad, that train station is really close."

Then our parents got busy and we learned to wait and disengage. Little by little, we stepped outside the window of our dreams and watched, the way we watch sports on TV instead of getting out there and playing. Without our parents realizing it, or our understanding it, our holograms started losing detail and feeling. And we started losing enthusiasm and power.

If You Don't Know What You Want, You Will Probably Get What Someone Else Wants

When you create dreams, here's the bottom line: *The more detailed your dream, the more power it has.*

In First Gear we learn to use other people's dreams, so our

dreams are only as powerful as the quantity and quality of detail they give us.

In Second Gear we test other people's dreams for ourselves, doubting, altering, shortcutting, rejecting—making them more and more detailed because of our growing interest and experience.

In Third Gear, we use all the sensory data we have been accumulating to create holograms of our own. We cut and paste, manipulate and alter, add and subtract—the way a graphic designer does using PhotoShop on a computer, or the way moviemakers do in a digital editing suite. Then our personally enhanced holograms begin attracting enhanced levels of information from other people and other sources, and our brains begin supplying us with hunches and ahas. We begin noticing connections we've never noticed. We find solutions we've never imagined before.

Whenever we find ourselves in new situations, we gear back. But how long do you stay in First and Second? Are you willing to shift into Third to begin creating exactly what you want? Or do you get stuck in a lower gear—without getting your result?

Lately I've been helping my daughter Margaret and my son-in-law transform the house they own into the "home of their dreams." Margaret is a board-certified neuroradiologist who makes life-and-death decisions every day by looking at what would seem to you and me like unclear images on film: Is this cancer or not? Is there a brain tumor present or not?

But when Margaret looked at her inner "image of home," it was too unclear to read, so she asked her husband to detail it with her. After weeks of waiting for him to schedule time to go shopping and with his encouragement, Margaret took on the project and headed for a well-respected furniture store that offered decorating services. Margaret told the decorator she wanted to be told exactly what to do. Relieved and feeling much safer, Margaret decided to make her decorator's plan her plan.

As the paint was being rolled on her bedroom wall, Margaret started questioning whether she liked what her decorator liked.

Deciding that she didn't, she moved on to another decorator, this time the owner of a small specialty shop. Margaret loved the way her room displays looked and felt in harmony with her taste at first. But it didn't take long before the details of the dream Margaret was creating and the details her second decorator were creating began to diverge.

By this time Margaret was beginning to realize that no one except Margaret knows what she wants—and it is up to her to explore, discover, and create what that dream looks, sounds, feels, smells, and even tastes like down to the last detail.

Creativity's certainty doesn't come from the outside. It is an evolving inner process that leads us to know that what we think and feel is true— true for us. Life is a process of discovering what we want and don't want, what we value and don't value. We take on others' ideas and values initially, testing and adjusting them, making mistakes and correcting them until we can create values of our own.

Highly successful people say that *life is a values'-clarification process.* Their failures, bankruptcies, and losses, wrong turns and corrections, refocusings and rebuildings, harsh words and sincere apologies, relationships lost and regained led them to the *truth* about *their* life and how they want to live it.

They realize that they have to allow those they lead—their children, students, and coworkers—to go through their own values-clarification process. They can lead by example, but a successful life has taught them that short-changing another person's value-forging, dream-making process is like trying to create stainless steel without heat. Something is created, but that something is less strong.

When What You've Been Taught Doesn't Work: Ahas and Breakthroughs

n Third Gear, you will learn to recognize hunches and ahas as gateways and guideposts. You will begin to embrace coincidence, serendipity, and chance. Many major discoveries occur by chance. A strange mold that formed in a Petri dish left less than clean yielded Penicillin. The English physician Edward Jenner happened to notice that milkmaids who had been infected with cowpox didn't contract smallpox. Aha! The smallpox vaccine was invented. Third Gear is a dream world—a world of holograms—a magical world even for scientists.

When the world-famous neurologist and physiologist Dr. Karl Pribram was a resident, he found himself in conflict. The more experienced he became, the more his experiences made him doubt what he'd been taught—that specific memories were stored in specific locations in the brain.

Pribram was seeing patients who'd had large parts of their brains destroyed, but they were *not* experiencing correspondingly large parts of memory loss. None of his patients ever reported forgetting a third of their jobs or families or anything else. Instead they remembered *everything*, but their memories were *hazy*. Instead of specific locations, Pribram reasoned, memories must be stored *throughout* the brain. But how?

We've all been in Pribram's shoes. We accept the validity of methods and theories we've learned until we begin using them, and suddenly we realize there are an ever-increasing number of exceptions. How many times have you sat at your desk, stood in your kitchen, or driven home wondering, Why am I doing this? This doesn't make sense. It would make more sense if . . .

The next step is far more exciting and magical! Aware or unaware, we begin searching. Let's step into Pribram's Third-Gear experience. As you try it on, you can begin recording in your brain what Third Gear looks, sounds, and feels like.

Holograms: The Aha Experience

In 1961, while thumbing through an issue of *Scientific American*, Pribram stumbled upon an article about something new—holograms. By now, you've seen holograms on credit cards, at Disney World, or when R2D2 projected a hologram of Princess Leia calling for galactic assistance in *Star Wars*. The princess appeared to be standing there, in not just two but three dimensions, looking, sounding, and pleading like a real princess.

What was it in that article that electrified Pribram and changed the direction of brain theory? When you cut up a photographic negative of, let's say, a tree, each part shows a part of the tree. But if you cut up holographic film, each piece shows the whole tree. A hologram (whole-o-gram) records the whole in each part: $\frac{1}{3}$, $\frac{1}{2}$, $\frac{1}{20}$, $\frac{1}{100}$—the smaller the part, the hazier the image. *Aha, that's it! Our brain stores memory holographically—whole in each cell.*

How Are Holograms and Memories Created?

Let's gear down to learn a little more about holograms. Why? Because once you learn how to create powerful thoughts, or holograms, instead of being pulled backward or sideways by other people's thinking or your own, your powerful created thoughts, or holograms, will attract you in the direction you want to go, ahead to your dreams.

How is a hologram created? To create a hologram, a laser beam is split. Part of the beam strikes the object (that part is called the object beam). The other part travels undisturbed to the film (that part is called the reference beam). The point where those beams intersect or *interfere* is recorded on film. When you look at holographic film, you don't see an object the way you do on a photo-graphic negative; instead you see a series of intersecting rings, or an interference pattern.

As coincidence would have it, just as I typed *interference pattern*, I heard rain coming down hard on my roof. Walking to the window, I looked out at my pond and there on the surface was a perfect representation of how exposed holographic film looks. As each raindrop fell, it created rings that rippled out and intersected with the rings from other raindrops. I chuckled as I realized what the universe had just provided. This is the way it is in Third Gear, if you are willing to notice!

Holograms are created using two or more laser beams. *Similarly memories are created using two or more laserlike inputs from your senses— seeing, hearing, touching, feeling, smelling, tasting, and doing.* Then, as you go about your life, incoming sensory beams instantaneously and unconsciously decode the interference patterns stored in your brain, allowing you to *recall* similar experiences, past and future. Just as you can holographically *reexperience* your past—you can go back and look around, you can listen to voices in the hall or coming from the kitchen, you can refeel old emotions—*you can preexperience desired futures as well. You can create "future memories."*

The more detailed ideas are, the more power they have.

The more senses are involved, the more power ideas have.

Thoughts actually generate an electromagnetic force field that attracts what you think. Some thoughts are measurably more powerful than others. Why? Because the more detailed your thoughts are, the more electromagnetic power they have. The more senses are involved—the more you can see, hear, feel, taste, and even smell what you're thinking—the more power thoughts have. *In fact, to create maximum attractive power, you will need to prelive your desired experience in as much multisensory detail as possible, the way you did when you were a child.*

We have been hologramming our whole lives, but we didn't realize it. The third Success Skill is about hologramming consciously.

Cy vs. Sy

For fifteen years I had been searching for an audiotape I heard once in the early 1980s. A few weeks after one of my seminars, a participant was listening to a weight-control program when she heard the narrator mention Pribram's name. Realizing this was probably something I would want to hear, she brought the tape over so we could listen to it together and I jotted down these words: "The hologram is a model of how visual and sensory information is received, stored, and recalled by the brain." Now all these years later, I longed to hear that tape again.

But all I could remember was the name of the company that produced it: Cybervision. Years ago I searched for a phone listing but, unable to find one, I suspended my search—until I woke up at 1:30 one morning thinking about that tape. Suddenly propelled by some new inner certainty, I jumped out of bed and started searching on-line. The first ten attempts yielded nothing, but on the eleventh, I was told to search for *SyberVision*! Next I was shown a long list of products about golf and tennis, but none rang a bell. Then I was shuttled off to an auction site that offered *SyberVision: The Neuropsychology of Weight Loss*. Aha! That was it. But there was only one copy left. There was a price to buy and one to bid, so I bought it immediately and let out a fifteen-year-long completion sigh as I headed back to bed and pulled up the covers with a smile on my face. In a matter of days the series that had eluded me for so long would be delivered to my door.

Fortunately the Internet searches not just by spelling but by association as well. In a flash I understood why I could never find that tape. My spelling was incorrect. It was SyberVision not Cybervision. *I had recalled that tape series using my audio track instead of my visual one. I had remembered what the word sounded like but not what it looked like.*

All these years later I remembered only one auditory element of that complex holographic memory, but as soon as I opened the Priority Mail package, I immediately recognized the black plastic, heat-sealed binder, the typeface of the white letters, the wide pink band around the top, the tone, pitch, and timbre of the narrator's voice, the feelings of excitement I felt when I heard Pribram's words, the details of the room in which I listened to that tape. I even remembered what my friend was wearing, how curly her hair was, how her perfume smelled, as well as how breathtaking the ocean looked from the window of my twentieth-floor condominium that day.

When memories are recorded in the brain, all the sensory inputs are laid down together. Like all those raindrops that hit my pond at the same time, all those sensory inputs are laid down across the brain at the same time, creating an interference pattern. When one detail is recalled, the other details come back as well.

The Reticular Activating System: Your Brain's Search-and-Find Mechanism

When you squeeze the last quarter inch of toothpaste out of the tube and mumble *I need toothpaste,* did you ever notice that the next time you are grocery shopping and headed down that aisle, toothpaste comes to mind? Perhaps a picture of toothpaste flashes in front of you or you hear yourself saying, *Oh yeah, I need toothpaste,* or you refeel that empty tube or the unique smell and taste of your favorite brand. Whichever set of sensory details triggers it, at just the right moment, you are reminded to take action. And you reach for that tube on the shelf and put it in your grocery cart.

Like a computer, your brain has a Find Command. But instead of searching for words and phrases, it searches for the external manifestations of the holograms you already have recorded in your brain. Moment by moment, twenty-four hours a day, your reticular activating system (the Razz) *compares* those details to the details of the data coming in through your senses (what you are seeing, hearing, feeling, tasting, and smelling) and alerts you when there are *similarities—opportunities to complete, delete, or create.*

Even if you are busy doing something quite different, your Razz is still searching and *alerting.* While you are sleeping, it sorts through the memories you recorded that day in search of incompletions, and it wakes you up in the night as you realize *I didn't tell . . . I didn't do . . . I forgot to call . . . I prelived that experience but I didn't complete it or delete it.* That Razz alert may leave you so adrenalized that you can't go back to sleep and you lie there for hours preliving what you're going to do when it's light enough to make phone calls and take action.

As you prelive a dream, you are programming those details in your Razz: The more detail your dream has, the more power it has. The more senses you preexperience, the more power your dream has. Then your Razz, automatically and unconsciously, monitors incoming sensory data as you go about your life.

Realizing Dreams: She Literally Married a Rocket Scientist

So far in your life you have laid down billions of holograms, lived and relived them, and reexperienced and reemphasized them, so it will take *skill* to move beyond them. Past memories are so highly detailed and multisensory that they attract more and more of the same. It takes a conscious effort to change direction. It takes not just *wanting* but the skill and patience to painstakingly construct a highly detailed future experience that will attract you in the direction you want to go now.

Judy's marriage was over—after three children, twelve years of her husband's addictions, broken promises, failed jobs, and that final scene when she saw him pick up their six-year-old by the shoulders and throw him on the bed in anger.

For weeks she had been imagining her desired future, listing and prioritizing hundreds of details about her next relationship. Then, in pursuit of a new career, she flew from Charlotte to Houston for a conference. There, in a room full of thousands of enthusiastic people—with no *conscious* thought of her list—she met Jonathan. They connected powerfully, at least on the surface. But how detailed was this match?

Returning to the shreds of her life and the challenge of unraveling and beginning again, she pushed ahead to divorce. Her husband moved out and she reconnected with Jonathan in writing:

"I feel as if I know you, but I don't. I only know what I have observed or intuited, and what you have chosen to reveal during our brief time together. But I'm being an adventurer, so here goes. I want to know you. I want to know what kind of car you drive, what political thoughts you have, what dreams and aspirations entice you, what confidences you haven't told a soul. And whether you would be willing to share them with me.

"If your answer is yes, let's set up a method of correspondence, telephone appointments or some regular way to keep in touch. It will be interesting to see whether I like you as much when I know you well, and vice versa. Even if you say *Stop! Go no further!* I hope you will feel I've added something significant to your life as well. Please answer swiftly, if only to relieve the suspense. You know, when I become as preoccupied with my business as I've become with this, I'll be rich!"

With half a country between them, week after week by phone or fax, they interviewed each other, sharing plans, preferences, fantasies, habits, strengths, and weaknesses. She sent him pictures of her with her kids, pictures of when she was fat, and pictures taken on rough mornings so he would know exactly what he would be getting. And he did the same as they explored the ins and outs of how their dreams and realities connected.

Finally, six months later, they met again on a beach in front of a sand dune. He handed her a rose and a twelve-times-folded note that read: "Judy Barner. You are the love of my life. I want to spend the rest of my life with you. Will you marry me?"

Experiencing and Remembering: Referring to and Deciding

o the brain, recorded past memories (holograms) and created future memories (holograms) are the same. Athletes use this information to great advantage. On TV we see them preexperiencing the perfect ski run, high jump, or golf shot. According to bestselling success writer Dr. Maxwell Maltz, "Experimental and clinical psychologists have proved beyond a shadow of a doubt that the human nervous system cannot tell the difference between an 'actual' experience and an experience imagined vividly and in detail."*

The more sensory details we create, the more power these created experiences have. Everyday language expresses this inner truth: I can see it now! I know exactly what she'll say! I know how it will feel. I want it so much I can even taste it! And, like a kid again, you get excited and powerful. *Wanting can be tricky, depending on where you stand when you're wanting.* If you stand inside your dream—inside the candy store enjoying that delicious candy—then that's the reality you will attract. But if you stand outside your dream—seeing others eating the candy but not you—then that is the reality you will attract. To manifest dreams you must detail them in advance and step into them *before* taking appropriate actions.

* Maxwell Maltz, *Psycho-Cybernetics* (New York: Prentice Hall, 1960), p. xi.

Try Your Hologram on Before
You Marry and Move In

Judy and Jonathan seemed perfect for each other, at least at the start. Their relationship flourished as they moved back and forth between lives and houses. So the idea of getting married and moving in together seemed like the logical next step. To her, he looked like a wonderful model for her two teenage sons. He was loving and gentle, an artist and craftsman. Together they enjoyed spontaneous moments and adventures, and she wanted her boys to have those experiences, too. To him, she and her sons looked like a perfectly sculpted family he could cherish. He had never had kids and he would simply step into her kids' lives. They would live in his house until they could find a new home.

When she and her two sons moved in, however, their lives didn't fit. He had never been around teenagers, and he didn't have the patience to live with two of them. What had looked great part-time interfered with his work and overwhelmed him financially. He had always lived minimally, spending extra money on exotic stone not exotic sneakers or computer games. The way her sons had been raised clashed with the way he'd been brought up. He was uncomfortable with what looked like too much freedom and too much stuff. Then suddenly a disastrous car accident landed them in the hospital and gave them time to think. And redecide.

He was in his house, but she had sold hers—the home in which she had raised her sons, the home in which she had invested years of mortgage payments—and buying a home of similar size and quality would cost far more today. After many painful hours, they created a new plan and, with courage, they prepared to support each other in moving ahead separately, as friends.

Moral of the story: Try on your holograms before you "marry and move into them." Test them out in your mind and body. If you discover that that reality is not what you want, then say no. Succeed by deleting.

How do you know when your hologram is detailed enough? Ideally it will be so detailed that if you walk all the way out to the end of the limb you are standing on, your next step will be so clear that you can safely and effortlessly step over. *Ideally your holograms are "real" to you before you take action.*

But most people jump into action before they gear up into creativity, so they spend their time feeling stuck and disappointed. Remember, actors memorize scripts and spend weeks practicing their parts and listening to other actors' parts, until they know them so well they are ready to step on stage and to transcend the script and allow other forces to take over.

Confusion: More Than One Hologram Per Dream

Sometimes you are clear but outside circumstances interfere with your clarity. Sharon hired a new secretary to manage her office, but between the time Sharon hired her and the time Candy reported to work, the political environment in Sharon's office changed drastically. Sharon's previous secretary, Beverly, failed to get another job as expected, and so she decided to play hardball to get her old position back. Weeks later, an unsuspecting Candy stepped into confusion. Instead of receiving messages that matched her interview impression, within a few days she was mired down in rumors that she didn't have a job; Beverly was coming back. So the surge of energy her new position had generated quickly dwindled to a mere trickle, barely enough to allow her to get up, get dressed, and go to work. Instead of focusing all her energies on learning what Sharon wanted, she was now forced to expend some of her energies on the question *What if...*

What is confusion? Let's look at the word: It comes from the Latin word *confusere,* which means "to fuse with." *When you have more than one hologram for the same experience—job, relationship, vaca-*

tion, instruction, or anything else—you experience confusion. The details of your holograms blur and overlap, or you are forced to switch back and forth between different ones. Bottom line, you are unable to direct enough energy to complete any of them. Highly successful people commit to one, and only one, hologram. And what you will need to be effective, efficient, and creative is the certainty of one, and only one, version of your dream.

Make sure all of your senses align. Some people show themselves wonderful pictures but tell themselves, "You can't. It will never happen." Or they have a gut feeling they're in for a disappointment. *Make sure you can see, hear, feel, taste, and smell yourself experiencing a successful outcome.*

The Positive-Command Brain: What You Think Is What You Get, Like It or Not

When I ask people *what they want,* more often than not they tell me *what they don't want.* But a hologram is a hologram; it's the same sensory complex whether stated positively or negatively. If you take the "not" out of the sentence, then you will discover exactly what the hologram is, and what result you'll probably get, like it or not.

Challenge yourself to listen for the "nots" in your life. What negative commands do you use unconsciously? What are you inadvertently dreading instead of dreaming? Don't forget to lock the door. Don't drink and drive. Don't use the elevator in case of fire. When you catch yourself giving negative commands, follow up immediately with positive commands: Remember to lock the door. Have someone else drive when you drink. In case of fire, use the stairs. *To succeed, we must give ourselves and others positive commands.*

Teachers and employers make the same error: Don't be late. Don't talk. Don't forget to . . . Lawmakers tell us what "not" to do and so do spouses and friends. Diets prescribe what not to eat and we eat it and regret it and never understand why. Here's why: To produce a result you have to create the experience you want and live it in advance in as much detail as possible. Prelive what you want. *You have a positive-command brain, and if you use it correctly, you can be successful and satisfied.*

Where do these negative commands come from? They are usually echoes from First- and Second-Gear instructions. Our parents and teachers and bosses were afraid for us, and they thought they were being protective, but by expressing their fears they hologrammed those fears in us and those fears are still there, blocking us. At this point those old holograms need to be updated.

His Mom Helped Him Build a Powerful, Positive Hologram

Instead of telling her son not to be afraid, Noah's mom stepped in to help him have a better experience in the present and lay down a better memory to refer to in the future. This is something we need to learn to do for ourselves, too.

When six-year-old Noah heard the doctor say he was going to have to walk across the street to have a blood test, his mind and body went into gear. If we had hooked him up to a blood pressure cuff, I'm sure we would have seen a measurable rise. Noah was imagining the excruciating pain he didn't want to feel, and he immediately told his mother, "No, not today," as though putting the test off until tomorrow would make it hurt less.

Then Noah's mom created a hologram: "Okay, here's the deal. If there are lots of people in line, we will come back tomorrow. But if there are only one or two, we'll save ourselves a trip and get it over with today." Noah agreed, and his mom went on to detail exactly what he should expect. "Will it hurt?" "Yes, a little," she said honestly, "but only for a second. Trust me, you'll be fine."

As they entered the antiseptic-smelling lab, to Noah's immediate horror, there were only two people waiting. He tightened up everything inside him to get through the ordeal. When his turn came, he squirmed and twisted to avoid the oncoming needle, and his mom helped his resolve by holding his arm still and repeating her holographic mantra: "Trust me, you'll be fine."

Just as the massive wall of anticipated pain should have hit, Noah let out a delighted yell. "Wow, the needle is in and it barely hurts at all. Look, Mom, I trusted you and you were right. I am fine." Why did Noah trust his mom? Because the hologram she helped him construct worked (his experience matched the details of the hologram she had helped him build). Next time he will be able to use that positive experience on his own.

We have been creating holograms our whole lives. Every memory we have is a hologram. Like Noah, we need to begin picking and choosing which ones we want to complete, delete, and create newly.

The Dream-Creating Question: What Do I Want?

In Third Gear, *What do I want?* becomes the key question; it is no longer a vague, far-off, conceptual question but a very specific question that you need to begin asking yourself moment to moment. What do I want for breakfast? What exactly do I want to communicate in this message or phone call? What do I want this product to do? What information do I want from this person or class? Asking these questions allows us to tune in to ourselves again.

As we begin in First Gear, "What do I want?" isn't the question on our minds. The question we keep asking is "What do you want?" In Second Gear, as we are producing and competing, the question we constantly ask our teachers and bosses is "What results do you want?" so we can climb *their* educational or corporate ladders and earn money, power, and position. But in Third Gear, we begin asking the dream-creating question "What do I want?" and in the process of answering that question day by day, we build dreams of our own that are so clear and detailed and thoroughly preexperienced that we recognize opportunities for next steps wherever we are. We are able to sense what each situation or person is contributing, what new angle, concern, or approach he or she is bringing to our awareness.

We Live in a Holographic Universe

The neurosurgeon Dr. Karl Pribram and the physicist Dr. David Bohm, as well as growing numbers of other scientists and philosophers, have come to the conclusion that our universe is a hologram; therefore we can never directly know it because we can only experience it through our senses.

Unlike King Midas, we don't turn everything we "touch" into gold, but we do turn everything we "sense" into what seems to be solid objects that exist in time and space. Pribram and Bohm challenge us to look more seriously at what the Eastern philosophers have been saying: Reality, at the highest level, is Maya. And what is Maya? Maya is simply a series of wavelike interference patterns, a series of holomovements and vortices.

In an interview in *Psychology Today,* Pribram said: "It isn't that the world of appearances is wrong; it isn't that there aren't objects out there, at one level of reality. It's that if you penetrate through and look at the universe with a holographic system, you arrive at a different view, a different reality. And that other reality can explain things that have hitherto remained inexplicable scientifically: paranormal phenomena, synchronicities, the apparently meaningful coincidence of events."*

* Quoted in Michael Talbot, *The Holographic Universe* (New York: HarperCollins, 1991), p. 271.

Shifting Levels of Reality:
A Sudden Glimpse into Another Time

I was visiting my friends Efrem and Harriet at their summer home in the mountains of northern California. After fifteen years in Miami, I was thrilled to revisit this wondrous wooded land, and I spent all afternoon walking alone and tuning in to plants I rarely see anymore—fuzzy mulleins and blue chicory growing along the roadside, the uniquely patterned barks of apple trees and pear trees. Later, as the evening light grew dim, Harriet and I were striding across a large open field, when I suddenly caught a sidelong glimpse of Native Americans in feathered headdresses dancing and drumming around a crackling fire.

Harriet noticed something unusual dart across my face and asked what had just happened. I told her about the Native Americans and the bonfire I had just seen. "Oh yes," she said, filled with awe, "that's sacred ground over there. That clearing is where the Klamath Indians used to hold their ceremonies." Somehow I had tapped into earlier sacred times on this land, where Harriet's "tribe" now holds their own earth-reconnecting rituals each year.

Is a dream, desire, or curiosity our key to entering other holographic realms of information, experience, and knowledge? When do coincidences seem to occur? When we have a carefully detailed, multisensory hologram in mind, and we take our attention off it to do something different and somehow we seem to step past our usual time, space, and experience limits into interconnectedness—into meeting, noticing, and realizing . . . into aha. Is an aha a glimpse into another realm, a momentary decoding of other levels of experience and knowledge? Did our hologram's electromagnetic force field attract that opportunity to us, and our attention to it?

Einstein said, "People like us who believe in physics know that the distinction between past, present and future is only a stubbornly persistent illusion." The distinction between future dreams and current realities is also a stubbornly persistent illusion. As we prelive experiences we encode that memory outside of time.

Maybe We Will Come to View Ourselves as "Web Browsers"

I can remember when there was only one channel available on TV. We watched the clock until it was time to see Howdy Doody, Milton Berle, or Jackie Gleason. Then came the days when we could receive two or three channels and that seemed like a luxury. Today we have eight hundred channels and more on demand. In another few years, when the availability of information is greater still via integrated TV and the Internet or some new technology as yet undiscovered, we will no doubt look back at how limited we are now.

The same process is going on within each one of us; remember, in a holographic universe, whatever piece we view contains the information of the whole. Perhaps we will find ourselves turning inward more and more, realizing we can tune to different frequencies and various levels of reality. Maybe we will come to see ourselves as "Web browsers" able to search for and locate more and more of what we want to know and experience. Maybe we will realize that we can go deeper and deeper into the multisensory holograms that we have created and that have been created by other people and other levels in the universe. Perhaps it is a matter of diving inward into wider and wider levels of existence and knowledge, and decoding those holograms so that we can use them now.

Can We Learn to Tap into Others' Holograms?

If the premise that we live in a holographic universe is true, it opens up the possibility that we can learn to access holographic information other than our own. Since the universe, as a hologram, would be whole in each part, then perhaps each of us is able to access universal knowledge.

Dr. Stanislav Grof, a psychiatrist at the Johns Hopkins University School of Medicine, started studying patients labeled as psychotic and paying close attention to the details of the "delusions" they were having. A follower of holographic theory, he had grown more and more interested in the possibility that these patients who were unable to stay in this reality were somehow tapping into another reality. And so he had his research team check up on the information his patients were describing. Amazingly, he was able to verify their information about ancestors and other places and times.

Wouldn't it be amazing if we could learn how to tap into not just the holograms in our own brains but the holograms of our ancestors as well? If we all began as one cell, then we have all potentially recorded not only the development of life but also the development of the universe.

That is a grand and wonderful possibility, which is being explored by both science fiction and science. From the cloning of Dolly the sheep to the current attempt to clone a woolly mammoth from one frozen for millennia deep underneath the Arctic ice, we are beginning to discover there is much more to explore and enjoy in our universe than we've ever known before.

Getting Help from Another Level

Are energies in other realms able to reach out to us? Just before Christmas four years ago, my friend Betty took temporary refuge in my home. She and her husband had just ended their ten-year marriage under very painful circumstances. She was feeling lonely and abandoned and I was having a hard time helping her through it all by myself.

On Christmas Eve, I was awakened in the early morning hours by an unusual voice: "Susan, I need your help." And there in front of me in the dim light was Betty's father-in-law, who had died several months before. "I need you to do something special for me. Tomorrow I want you to find a Jewish star to give to Betty for Christmas. It needs to be old and silvery like me," he chuckled, "but alive and sparkly like her. Please wrap it and put in a note: 'Merry Christmas to Betty from Lou.' Please be sure to tell her I love her . . . now and always. And I am proud of the openness to Judaism she has shown our family."

I was startled by his extraordinary visit, and I felt very fortunate that I had met Lou once before he died. Delighted to do this for Betty and Lou, I had no idea how on Christmas Eve I would find that old, silver, sparkly Jewish star he described. I busied myself with other tasks until I got an electric-charged feeling that I had to go to a consignment shop a few blocks away. I knew it was a long shot because they sold clothing, but I was way past thinking logically at that point and I had such an urgent feeling that I got in my car. And there in a glass case, buried under a bunch of papers, was exactly what Lou had described—a silver marquisette Jewish star the owner said a young woman had left on consignment the day before.

On Christmas morning, as everyone else unwrapped presents, Betty was obviously sad until I told her to look for a small box with her name on it under the tree. With a shocked but delighted glance, she went over and retrieved it. Sitting down, she began reading the note aloud. I had told everyone else what to expect so the room fell silent in awe as she clutched Lou's star to her heart and I told her about his visit.

Divorce or no divorce, Betty no longer felt alone and abandoned. Somewhere in another realm the man she considered her true father was with her. And for months after that, whenever the pain of her disrupted life overtook her, she would hold Lou's star to her heart and he was there.

"When we experience a synchronicity," writes theoretical physicist F. David Peat, "what we are really experiencing is the human mind operating, for a moment, in its true order and extending throughout society and nature, moving through orders of increasing subtlety, reaching past the source of mind and matter to creativity itself."* To enjoy our creativity, we must be able to trustingly step out on a limb and beyond. We must let go of past limits and logic and move into the unknown.

Third Gear is about choosing what we want and creating powerful "future memories" that attract those experiences to us. Like playwrights and movie directors, we are creating our own lives. Will we continue to use the billions of memories we laid down unconsciously, or will we begin to choose which holograms we entertain in our minds and start attracting those experiences instead? With the hologramming skill in place, you have a choice.

Whether we are scientists breaking new ground, actors stepping into store windows to explore career possibilities, inventors sourcing products and technologies, or individuals breaking through into consciously living our dreams day to day, we would do well to remember the advice actor Anthony Hopkins gave to a nervous student: "Be bold and mighty forces will come to your aid."

Success-Filing your "potential successes": It's time to add another cluster of successes you can acknowledge for yourself. What powerful holograms did you create today or sometime in the past? What did those holograms alert you to do? What opportunities came your way as a result? What changes to old holograms did you make today? What details did you add or subtract? Which future holograms did you prelive?

---

* F. David Peat, *Synchronicity: The Bridge Between Mind and Matter* (New York: Bantam Books, 1987), p. 235.

Communicating
So Powerfully

n Skill 3, you detailed your dream as much as you could on your own. In Skill 4 you will detail your dream as much as possible with your Codreamers, which will allow you to experience your dream from more angles and perspectives. After all, you are creating a whole-o-gram.

With your dream well formed, you are seeking people who will believe in your dream with you, contribute detail and power to it, and wake up in the middle of the night with an insight to share. You are seeking people who will keep your dream alive if you abandon it—and even reinstall it in your brain if circumstances "erase" it.

You are reaching out to people who are willing to navigate the bends, bumps, and obstacles with you, who are more committed to your dream than to your fears or theirs. People who will eagerly await your phone call after an important meeting—or call if you don't. You are searching for people who will savor your successes in the hall, over lunch, by E-mail or phone, people who will joyously celebrate your dream's completion: "Remember when you first told me . . . Remember when you couldn't . . . Remember when they wouldn't . . . Remember when you realized . . ." Until finally one day, "Hey, look at us now. We are standing in your dream!"

At this point in the success process you are *not* looking for people to lend you money, decorate your home, run your sales department, or set up your Internet site. At this point, you are *not* looking for people to *do* anything. You are seeking a foundation for your success. You are seeking people who will dream with you. You may have a short list of people you think will be the most likely candidates, but sometimes Codreamers turn out to be the people you least expect.

Starting Over: Creating Holograms and Integrating Old Ones

Today Carlos is a highly successful international real-estate broker, but when he was just out of college and desperate for freedom, the first drug deal he attempted landed him in prison. Everyone who knew him was shocked—such a smart kid from such a good family. But that was only how it looked from the outside.

His busy mother and father never had time for him as a boy. His doctor-father dragged him to the hospital and plopped him at the nurses' station for hours on end. His socialite mother didn't listen when he protested he didn't want to go with her to the hairdresser again. When he was four, he threw himself in their swimming pool, hoping to die. His older cousin fished him out, and his mother yelled at him endlessly for making her late.

After two years in prison, he was finally free. But no matter how hard he tried, he kept slipping back into old patterns. Once I explained holograms to him, Carlos understood why his highly detailed past experiences kept pulling him back—and why his dreams would need to be far more detailed to attract him ahead. Week after week, in as much multisensory detail as I could press him to generate, Carlos imagined his new life, laying down new interference patterns across his brain and mine. Carlos visualized living up high in a spacious home overlooking aqua ocean all the way to the horizon. He prelived running his own firm and talked me through interactions with clients, even "reading" me appreciation letters he had framed in his study. Now aware of his old compulsion to want too much too soon, he emphasized how it felt to be patiently and meticulously building a new life.

The Woman of His Holograms

Next he started dreaming about a wife—what she would be like, her personality and interests. He saw her coming from a Mediterranean country, heard her speaking multiple languages, and felt himself being welcomed into her warm, supportive family. Carlos described what weekdays would be like and what they would do on weekends and holidays—how well they were aligned on plans and priorities.

Once Carlos's dream was well formed, he began selectively sharing it with family and friends. First he described his "wife," hoping someone might pass on her phone number or, better yet, introduce them. Meanwhile he continued completing degrees and licenses, acquiring skills and connections; he volunteered for community projects and was invited to step into leadership.

Months later, Carlos's mother called to say she had just met "the woman of his holograms." She had just moved here from Spain. She was probably single and definitely beautiful and didn't know a soul. His mother urged Carlos to drive over and introduce himself right away.

On a Monday morning three weeks later Carlos finally followed through, inviting Catherina for coffee. That Saturday they played tennis and enjoyed a long, leisurely dinner, but when they said good night, she made it clear she had a boyfriend in Boston. Over the next few months, they spent time together as friends.

Instead of Fast-Forwarding to the End, Let's Pause to Look Closer

I could skip over all the other parts of Carlos's story you might need to know at this point: the times his past overwhelmed him and broke down his confidence; the extra steps he was required to take to earn licenses; the belt-tightening days when there was nothing in his refrigerator because the commission check he was owed, and desperately needed, was tied up in administrative red tape. I could *not* tell you about the morning Carlos asked his dad if he could move home for a while. His father had said yes and Carlos planned accordingly, but three days later Carlos's mother decided no, leaving him in a worse jam.

You need to know that these interferences won't just come from outside. Once Carlos's hologram was clear, other voices inside him started interfering, too: "Yeah, but that's ridiculous. How can you dream about living perched high above the beach when you don't have two nickels to rub together? You must be crazy!"

Even after Carlos's mother provided his future wife's name, address, and phone number, it took him three weeks to take action. Why? Because he was caught up in other holograms, old and new: "My mother stomped out every childhood dream I ever had and I'm not going to let her do it to me again. Besides, I've got too much to do to go on a wild-goose chase right now." For three weeks Carlos experienced so much internal resistance that he couldn't take action and when he did, his dream was interfered with again: "But I have a boyfriend in Boston."

I share Carlos's story in depth at this point because these are the details you may not know about highly successful people.

These details usually don't show up in a résumé, five-minute TV profile, or background blurb you are handed about your boss. These details are usually kept hidden from your view, giving you the false impression that highly successful people don't encounter the same dilemmas you do, or worse. But omitting these details now would distort your whole-o-gram.

Remember, most success stories are shared from a First- or Second-Gear perspective; they are constructed to build your confidence in that person or aimed to prove how productive and competitive he or she is. Most success stories are not designed to give you a realistic, day-to-day sense of what to expect as you shift into Third Gear and head for your dreams.

Picking Up the Story Again

Just before Christmas, Catherina flew home to Spain to spend the holidays with her family and Carlos was shocked to discover how lonely he felt with her a continent away. A few days later she called to say she was ill and would need to stay longer. Suddenly Carlos found himself grabbing pen and paper and writing a long list of reasons he missed her. Then—driven by this new inner something—he rushed out to buy a fuzzy bear he overnighted to Spain to "hand deliver" his list. On his way home, as his adrenaline subsided, Carlos caught himself musing, "I've never done anything like that before. I must be in love." Arriving in Spain, the bear delivered his message straight to her heart. And a month or so later, the boyfriend in Boston became just a friend.

Three years later, my mailman handed me an elegantly engraved invitation for Carlos and Catherina's wedding, which was to be celebrated in Spain. Unable to attend, I was invited to visit their home when they returned. As Carlos's Codreamer, that was quite a moment for me. I was covered with goose bumps as I stepped into that high, sunny, aqua-ocean-surrounded space, recognized Catherina, and savored pictures of their wedding. As I walked around their home, I saw Carlos's framed degrees and appreciation letters on the wall of his study. I was standing in the dream Carlos and I had been codreaming for years. Carlos's dream had become his reality, Catherina's, and mine.

Preparing to Find Codreamers

When I read this story to Carlos, he chuckled. "The parts you included are true, but the parts you didn't include were most essential. If I hadn't been Success-Filing, if I hadn't known which Success Gear people were in, if I hadn't had a detailed dream and other people dreaming it with me—and sometimes even for me—I would have believed the voice in my head that constantly shouted: 'Your past will hold you back.' But with these skills in mind, I was able to shout back even louder—'You just wait and see!'"

Are you practicing the skills we have covered so far? *Skill 1:* Success-File each day to build and maintain your self-confidence. *Skill 2:* Take time to recognize which Success Gear people around you are in. *Skill 3:* Detail and redetail your dream as you integrate new ideas, yours and others'. Using these skills will prepare you for when fears, opinions, judgments, arguments, persuasions, pressures, and loudly shouted oppositions start coming at you.

When Carlos started sharing his hologram, he was selective. Why? Because not everyone you share your dream with will amplify it; some people will diminish it, planting fresh doubts or reinforcing old ones: "With your background, Carlos, who are you kidding?"

Some people will try to convince you to give up before you start. Others will do their best to turn you back somewhere along the way. Exactly where? you ask. At exactly the point where *they*—or, in their minds, any "sane person"—would turn back. "This dream is taking too long. And you're still not making money. Enough is enough!"

Not everyone you share your dream with will be comfortable in Third Gear—and you may not be either. Most people spend their time in First and Second. In First Gear we were taught to withhold information for rightness' and politeness' sake; in Second Gear we learned to withhold and distort details for competition's sake; but in Third Gear, as creators, we can no longer hold back. *For the first time we must commit to having our hologram and others' as close to one and the same dream as we can possibly make them.*

Computer Hackers: Beware *and Be Aware of Sensory Fill-In*

Warning: At this point in its development, your dream will be sketchy, so other people will automatically and unconsciously begin completing your sketch for you—adding their own details and erasing some of yours. I call this process *Sensory Fill-In.*

At the end of some conversations you may feel like a computer hacker has gained entry to your brain and graphically manipulated the sensory details you had stored there so that your dream no longer looks, sounds, or feels like it's yours. When you sense what's going on, you may want to shout: "Hey, wait just a minute! This is my dream you're changing." And it may take a few days to feel like its creator-owner again.

But it is important to realize that some of the details others fill in may be useful and even brilliant. And once you regain your balance, you can sort through their changes to see which ones you want to include and which ones you want to delete. But all of those details, whether you decide to include them or not, will help you communicate your dream more effectively the next time.

When you send someone to the store to buy toothpaste, you may be sadly disappointed when you open the bag and the toothpaste they bought for you isn't your brand or size or flavor or cap style. It's the brand, size, flavor, and cap style they would buy for themselves. *To avoid Sensory Fill-In, we must challenge ourselves to communicate as much multisensory detail as possible up front.* All that fuss about which toothpaste may sound silly, but if that trip to the store is going to be a success for both of you, then both of you must have the same hologram in mind. The power of communication is in the details. Whether it's toothpaste, decorating, parenting, or implementing a business plan, check to be sure all of you have the same dream in mind before taking action.

How can you make your way through these communication obstacles and strengthen your dream in the process? The first step is to have people play back *what they think you said.*

Record and Play Back: How Do You Know When Someone Is Codreaming?

Your first responsibility as a communicator is to make time to share the details of your hologram and have those details played back to you. Then you can see, hear, and feel slight or gross additions, subtractions, alterations, and holes. You can communicate your hologram again, clarifying details and filling in holes until "what you have in mind" and "what they have in mind" are as close to the same dream as you can possibly make them.

If you fail to spend time getting the details aligned, then you will have created the errors that result: "I thought I showed you. . . . I meant to tell you. . . . I thought you knew. . . . That was what you told me last time. . . ." Other people's questions and differences press you to create and communicate your hologram in far greater detail.

When their hologram and your hologram match as far as is humanly possible, you have re-created yourself out there in the world. You have multiplied your electromagnetic force field. The more people who have your highly detailed hologram in mind, the more likely you are to succeed—and the more likely they are to succeed along with you.

Communicate Your Dream into the Razzles of as Many People as You Can

In Skill 3 you learned that the Razz is the part of your brain that alerts you to matches between your hologram and the data coming in through your senses. When you prelive your holograms with other people and they record and play them back accurately, you program their reticular activating systems as well. Then, as they go about their lives, they will automatically and unconsciously monitor their incoming sensory data for details of your dream as well as their own, multiplying your opportunities for success.

How many reticular activating systems does your dream prelive in? How many people's dreams do you prelive in yours? When was the last time you passed on a middle-of-the-night realization or an aha, or had one passed on to you?

Lies and Distortions: Manipulating the Details of Holograms

We tell the truth when we accurately represent the hologram we have in mind. We lie when we distort the details of the hologram we are communicating—making it seem larger or smaller, harder or easier, sooner or later, more or less acceptable, requiring more or less action or effort. When we distort holograms, other people operate on inaccurate information, resulting in mistakes, injuries, scheduling snafus, unplanned destinations, unfulfilled expectations, upsets, arguments, distrust, and disillusionment.

We lie in an attempt to get something we want—a favor or help, trust or respect, power or position, money or fame—that we don't believe people will give us if we tell them "our truth." Beneath lying is a deep-seated and culturally taught belief that the truth is not enough, that we should feel and behave differently than we do. This worldview, which we learned in First and Second Gears, keeps creating upsets.

Word Cues and Eye Signals

Pay close attention to your eyes as you follow these instructions: Take a minute to think about a home you lived in years ago. *Picture* it in as much detail as possible. Count how many windows you can see as you walk room to room. Recall the *sounds* you heard when you lived there—kitchen sounds, street sounds, laughter, conversations, radio, stereo, or TV. Notice your eyes. Which way did they move?

When the sensory-cue words—*see, watch, observe, notice*—signal you to search *visually,* your eyes move up and to the right, or you seem to see those details a few feet in front of you. When the sensory-cue words—*listen, hear, sound*—tell you to switch into audio, your eyes automatically and unconsciously move toward your right ear, switching your brain into audio. Think about how you *felt* and *what you did* when you were living in that home. Recall happy moments, birthdays and holidays, or how many steps you had to climb up to your front door. What happens to your eyes now? In this search mode, your eyes move down toward your body.

Bottom line, your eyes move up to see, ear to ear to hear, and down toward your body to remember feelings and actions. Your eyes move right to search the past and left to create the future.

These eye signals alert us to how precise our communications must be. When people ask you what something *looks like,* they are adding, subtracting, or altering details in their visual track. When they ask what someone said or what something *sounds like,* they are recording details in their sound track. When they ask what something *feels like* or *what they need to do,* they are working in their feeling-doing or kinesthetic track. To communicate effectively, to create trust and alignment, you need to operate in the specific sensory mode they request. And they need to do that for you.

Do you hear me? Yes, I hear you. Do you see what I mean? Yes, I see what you mean. Do you have a feel for how this works? Yes, I have a feel for it. Do you know what to do? Yes, I know what to do now.

You Won't Feel a Thing: Creating Trust or Distrust

When what we are told and what we experience match, then trust and cooperation are created. But when they don't match, fear and upset result. Fred Rogers, creator of Mister Rogers' Neighborhood, remembers only too well how frightened he felt as a shy only child confronting new situations. So he composed a song called "I Like to Be Told" to help today's kids know what to expect when they first flush a toilet or go to a doctor or dentist. And the child in each one of us wants to know what to expect, too.

Lying in my dentist's chair with my paper bib still clipped on after a cleaning, I was relieved to hear my hygienist say, "Everything looks fine. The doctor will be right in to check you." But after a warm hello and a few unanticipated groans and grimaces, he announced that I needed a bone graft on one of my left lower molars. Shocked, I asked him to explain the procedure and he talked me through it step by step, using detailed pictures of what he would do when and why. Satisfied that I understood the surgical procedure, I then asked him about the experience I would have as a patient. What would I feel? What would the recovery be like?

How much pain would I have? His answer was satisfying in that moment: "You won't feel a thing." And once I was numb, I felt a lot of pressure but I didn't feel pain as he ground out diseased bone around the root of my tooth and packed in new bone from a generous cow donor.

It was what he didn't tell me that created the upset. He didn't tell me that three days later I might experience a great deal of swelling and intense pain; I might not be able to sleep or eat comfortably for two weeks; I might not be able to focus for almost three weeks. So when those unspoken "mights" turned into reality, I was unprepared to deal with the dilemma they created.

My support team and I had started updating my computer system a few days before the surgery, and we were half out of the old system and half in the new with no place to go but ahead. Now, postsurgery, I found myself struggling to learn things I couldn't learn with these hot, throbbing sensations blazing in my head day and night. If I had been given a more accurate hologram up front, I would have postponed the surgery until we had completed the computer project.

Now this dentist is someone the child in me doubts because he failed to communicate accurately what life might be like during those three weeks. And you can be sure the next time he describes a procedure, I will ask others what their experience was like.

How well did I fulfill my responsibility to myself in this communication? Did I ask enough questions? Did I spell out how critical the next few weeks were for me? Did I ask whether the surgery could be postponed until we finished the conversion? Or did I get swamped by the authority of his message and gear back into childlike acceptance?

The word *integrity* comes from the Latin word *integer,* which means whole or entire. We experience integrity when the hologram we *attempt* to create in someone else's mind aligns detail for detail with the one we have in mind. On the other side of communication, we experience integrity when the hologram someone *attempts* to create in our mind aligns detail for detail with the experience we then have.

I emphasize the word *attempt* because people rarely record the exact words we use and, even if they do, those words take on different meanings when they're instantaneously and unconsciously compared with *their* experiences, past and future. We may appear to be working together but without carefully aligned holograms we may be working apart, pulling in opposing directions and canceling out each other's energies.

What can we do about this holographic communication gap? When we record a message on an answering machine, we play back our message so we can experience it ourselves. We consider our words, tone, pace, volume, enthusiasm—or our lack of it—and if that message isn't the one we want to send, we record and play it back until it is right. Similarly, when we record a message in another person's sensory system, we need to ask them to play back the message they received so we can provide additional details and explanations and so we can resolve differences before we take action. We are responsible for making sure they are cocreating our dream.

Remember, communication increases your hologram's attractive power. And playback increases the probability that you and your Codreamers are attracting the same thing!

His Wife Wouldn't Dream with Him

Skill 4 is about finding people with whom to share dreams. Ideally they're your marriage partners and friends, but that's not always the case. When does it become clear that someone is simply not interested in dreaming with you and you need to move on to find a Codreamer?

Jason and Sandra created a beautiful wedding on the beach and built, furnished, and landscaped two multimillion-dollar homes, but when it came time to talk about children, Sandra simply wouldn't participate. Jason wasn't sure what was wrong, so they kept taking courses and planning exciting trips together. From outward appearances, everything looked fine, but Jason was feeling worse.

Already in his mid-forties, Jason felt his days for raising a family were running out. He thought perhaps the reason Sandra wouldn't dream with him was because he wasn't communicating effectively, so he asked me for help. Together we detailed his dream, recording and playing it back until it was perfectly clear he was sending his dream skillfully. Then he went home to share his dream with his wife. But like a tape that needs to be turned over, whenever he put his hologram into his wife's head, she ejected it.

After a few days, she mustered up the courage to tell her husband "her truth." She knew exactly what his hologram was; he had communicated it effectively. The reason she wouldn't dream about having children with him was because she didn't want to parent with him. She wanted a divorce.

Not all messages you send will be received; some convey dreams other people don't want to cocreate. When you know your communication is clear, when you've presented your message over and over, then you will either have to let go of your dream—in this case, having children—or have to let go of codreaming it with that person. Confronting the whole truth, Jason and Sandra chose to go their separate ways, and now they are enthusiastically creating families with other partners.

Remember, success is completion and it's also deletion. There are other Codreamers out there if you are willing to start searching again, but some people choose to stay stuck—I want this dream and it has to include this person, this job, this house, or this city—and, disregarding low energy, depression, and illness, they remain incomplete and unsatisfied.

Here are some questions to ask yourself: If I abandon this dream, will I destroy myself? If I follow this dream, will I have to let go of this relationship? Or, if I remain in confusion, will I destroy both?

Letting go of the details of a long-held dream—and creating new details—is one of the most emotionally challenging things we ever have to do in life. Most people prefer to gear back into argument, pressure and persuasion, right and wrong, good and bad, blame and resentment. Or they decide to distort the details of what they tell themselves and others in a futile attempt to have it both ways, thereby disempowering themselves and creating mistrust and misalignment.

Hothousing Your Dream: Whose Input to Include and Whose to Exclude

f people say your dream is impossible right off the bat, then what they are telling you is they can't be Codreamers. If you accept too much First-Gear input, it will simply throw you back into First Gear. If you accept too much Second-Gear input, it will kick you back into Second Gear. Remember, you are operating in Third Gear, and this is your dream. And you are responsible for keeping it alive and growing.

Just as you protect a tiny seedling in a greenhouse until it is ready to transplant, you will need to keep your dream hothoused for a while. At this point in its development, your dream needs extra care and protection. You fertilize your dream by experiencing it from as many angles as possible with people who are committed to its survival and not its death.

You will start hearing all the reasons why not as soon as you begin asking people not just to think with you, but to commit their time, energy, money, and expertise to your dream (Skill 5). Understanding others' fears and doubts will be useful then. Understanding others' concerns about time, money, and systems will be important then. But right now you're looking for "the keepers of your dream"—you are searching for Codreamers wherever you can find them.

Ideally you will seek out as many people in Third Gear as you can. But just because someone is in Third Gear in one area doesn't mean that he or she will be there in your area. And when you guess wrong and others' input swamps you temporarily, go someplace alone and replay your dream. Or ask a Codreamer to play back your dream for you. Relive its possibility—relive all the reasons why this is your dream.

She Needed to Know the Truth, but What Was It?

Ronnie's life with Howard always revolved around work. Shortly after they met they started building a construction business. For years it had been exciting and astoundingly profitable, but after the birth of their first child, a new reality set in. As Ronnie began picking up more of *their* responsibilities at home, Howard wasn't picking up more of *her* responsibilities at work, and no one else was either. Ronnie was worried.

When Howard and Ronnie first went for counseling, she was hugely pregnant with their second child. Despite assurances that he would slow down and help more at home, Howard was still behaving as though he didn't have kids. Ronnie was nearing her breaking point, trying to handle her workload and her mother-load, too.

Once their son arrived, they started searching for a larger home. Howard wanted to continue accelerating their mortgage debt by acquiring more land and amenities that Ronnie would be responsible for. But Ronnie wanted to slow down, so she and the kids went to spend a relaxed month with her parents.

While Ronnie was away, she received a call from a coworker

who said he had information about her husband if she wanted it. Torn, she said yes, and he told her he had seen Howard kissing a friend's wife in a parking lot at three in the morning. He described the car Howard had been driving and asked if she knew a woman whose initials were BLC. With a horrifying inner thud, she acknowledged that she did.

Now, seriously doubting something she had never questioned before, Ronnie became an investigator. Reviewing her husband's cell phone bills, she discovered that he had been placing fifteen to twenty calls a week between the time she thought he was leaving work and the time he usually arrived home late. Howard had even been on the phone the morning their daughter had broken her arm at school and he was late getting to the hospital. Ronnie was enraged, disoriented, and confused. Suddenly the holograms of their life and marriage shifted and blurred, and she could no longer see a clear picture.

"The Truth" in First Gear

Ronnie begged Howard to tell her what he and that woman had been discussing, what needs this woman was meeting that she wasn't. If he told her "the truth," she felt she could forgive him.

But Howard had grown up in a First-Gear, people-pleasing reality, where "the truth" was "whatever his parents and teachers wanted him to say." Where men told wives what they thought would stop them from complaining and nagging—without having to change their own actions. So for Howard, "the truth" always started with *"but . . .":* "But you know I'd never do anything like that." "But you know she is someone I do business with." "But you're just getting yourself all upset over nothing."

In that moment Ronnie wanted to believe her husband so

much that she couldn't bring herself to ask him the question she needed an answer to, and she was amazed when their counselor simply asked, "Howard, have you had sex with anyone else since you've been married?" And he said yes and started answering Ronnie's questions one by one. With this "unacceptable" part of the hologram out of the bag, with his old limits to the truth taken down, they were ready to commit to "the whole truth"—a shared truth. They were ready to begin rebuilding their trust and their marriage.

"The Truth" in Second or Third Gear Is Just as Difficult

A highly competitive lawyer, Mark is constantly pressed for time, rushing from meeting to meeting and trying to keep up with the never-ending stream of phone calls and E-mails he receives every day, buffeted by one urgent matter after another. So to "make time," he tells his wife that he's leaving the office when he still has a phone call to make. She's on her way home from work, too, trying to juggle reconnecting with their four-year-old, dropping off their nanny, and starting dinner. The second time she calls, he tells her he'll be home in thirty minutes, even though he is just unlocking his car in the parking lot at work, knowing it will take him forty-five minutes to drive home even with no traffic, of which there is plenty at this hour. And then, when he pulls up in the driveway and she's obviously furious, he blows up at her for nagging. No matter how many times she asks him to tell her "the truth," he still *stretches* time in the name of getting everything done.

Then there is Tom, so concept oriented no one can ever get down to brass tacks with him. His ideas are brilliant; his new technologies are amazing. But his sales team, which came on board in awe, is now afraid to promise a customer anything, knowing they will be the ones who will have to handle their complaints while Tom tweaks his latest technology, perfecting one last version or performing one last trial, as once again his dream fails to become their customers' reality in time to be useful. No matter how much they sell, they can't make a living with Tom as their boss.

The issue here is communication. To take your dream from thought to reality, you will need to communicate and cooperate with people in all three gears. Then, when the phone rings and someone needs directions, or your child needs you to set limits, or your spouse calls all revved up in Second Gear to ask a last-minute favor, you will need to be able to shift your communication down or up accordingly to get in synch with each other. You may want to say to yourself, "Okay, now I need to shift gears." And then give yourself a second or two to reorient before you begin communicating in First, Second, or Third Gear, whichever is appropriate.

Actions Speak Louder Than Words

Even with the best intentions, old habits sometimes overtake us. We know we need to tell "the truth." We know we've made agreements, but we simply go on automatic and fail to follow through.

Justine had surgery when she was sixteen, and her doctor told her she would never have children. So when she found out she was pregnant years later, it was nothing short of miracle—but an unexpected one. Nine months later she and her boyfriend had a baby before they had a relationship. Loving their daughter, they were learning to love each other.

When Justine and Joseph's daughter was almost two, he bought a beautiful anniversary card and added a note: "Let's spend this special day together." Justine was excited. Their life together had been anything but romantic. She had spent most of her pregnancy flat on her back, missing her energetic lifestyle and straining their finances. During those months, their communication was rocky.

Everything they said seemed to trigger upsets and insecurities they didn't know how to resolve. So this card was a treasure Justine read and reread.

Their anniversary with two-year-old Debbie was hectic as usual—breakfast, laundry, play, and cleanup. Midmorning Joseph had a call from a friend who needed help for a couple of hours and—after saying yes—he turned to Justine for her okay. Justine nodded a numb yes.

But once Joseph left, she was furious. Once again he had put his friends first. The whole time he was gone, she tortured herself—it was a beautiful card, but he didn't mean a word of it. When his "couple of hours" turned into all afternoon, she sobbed on his return, "Special day together. Ha!"

Later they sat down together to rethink what had happened. After recording and playing back over and over, they were able to see solutions they hadn't noticed at the time. Together they created holograms for what to do next time: talking over their day *as soon as* they got up; checking with each other *before* making other agreements; and telling the whole truth about how they were feeling *in the moment.*

Do you say the right things and then not follow through with the right actions: I'll call you back in five minutes. I'll invite them to come, too. The gift is in the mail, or is it the check? Do you hear yourself each time you say something untrue? Do you feel the jolt of deception or exaggeration inside you, or do you no longer notice?

Here is an exercise you can do to eliminate broken agreements and upsets. *For two weeks, do everything you say you'll do, when you say you'll do it—even if it means staying up all night.* During those two weeks, you will learn to cut down on promises and say no more often. Then people around you will know what they can count on you for, and you will immediately set them free to find other ways to do the rest.

Upsets Disappear When You Play Them Back Completely

Logic might tell you the fastest way to solve an upset person's problem is to fix that problem. But it isn't. Why? Because once someone is upset, there are two problems that need to be solved: the upset they're stuck with—and the original problem. Solve the upset first. Why? Because when you rewind a person's experience, like rewinding a videotape, you come to the upset first. So that's the problem you need to complete first.

What should you do to assist an upset mate, coworker, or customer? *Let the person express their feelings fully—without interruption—and play them back in detail.* Then the upset will be released, usually with an apology: "Sorry. I didn't mean to take my upset out on you." Once the upset is expressed completely, you can rewind to the initial problem and begin to solve it.

Most people don't listen to upset people's experiences. Instead they rush into solution, disagreement, and argument. *But when you block their upset feelings, they turn them on you and everyone else they encounter,* until someone finally slows down long enough to really listen and re-create their whole-o-gram. Make sure you take the next step as well—continue to make that correction in the future.

Getting the "Whole Story" in a Mass-Marketing World

With the mass use of print, radio, TV, and the Internet, our need to communicate with integrity is far greater. High-tech computer graphics, multimillion-dollar production studios, TelePrompTers, and professionally edited messages enable us to present our ideas in greater detail. We communicate powerful holograms each time we create an ad or a commercial to program someone to spend time and money to meet a real need or a holographically induced one, and each time we portray a person as a hero or villain, attractive or unattractive, successful or unsuccessful.

We must create integrity in high-tech communications as well, appreciating the power these detailed, multisensory messages carry and anticipating the behavioral impact they have. A TV show can program audiences to unconsciously believe that all family crises, legal battles, and medical emergencies can be handled in an hour minus commercials. Viewers are entertained but then unprepared when these situations take far more time and effort to resolve. And these detailed, multisensory messages overwhelm our children, who have not yet had enough time to create sufficiently powerful holograms of their own to enable them to sort through and integrate the compelling details they are receiving.

How Else Do We Communicate?

In our holographic universe thoughts are constantly being transmitted and received. We are just beginning to explore the power of thought, whether the thought is a prayer or a clearly sent mental image. In sleep studies at Maimonides Hospital in Brooklyn, New York, one person, referred to as a "sender," focused his or her attention on the details of a different painting each night. Simultaneously in another part of the hospital, the "receiver" was sound asleep, and each morning he recorded detailed descriptions of what he had dreamed. Were the details of the paintings— colors, moods, people, scenes—that showed up in his dreams merely a chance occurrence? Not likely—the probability of that happening was calculated to be one in a million! Holographic communication is taking place in ways we currently don't understand: telepathy, dreams, ESP. Hospital studies have shown that healers can lower the blood pressure of cooperating patients, regardless of distance. As science advances, what more will we discover about how we communicate?

Five hundred years ago the idea that sound waves could be sent through the air over great distances seemed preposterous. A century ago the idea that pictures and sounds could be transmitted through air, walls, and bodies, and reassembled in picture tubes in living rooms, cars, and planes was preposterous. Maybe a few years in the future we will take for granted that pictures, sounds, feelings, tastes, smells, and even body movements are being electromagnetically transmitted and received by the brain.

Researchers have already shown that people talking on the phone in different locations move their arms and bodies responsively as they communicate. *When we intend to communicate, we do.* Or, as my grandmother used to say, Where there's a will, there's a way. Whether we are working to teach concepts to a child or reinstall the dream of a Codreamer, we need to begin opening ourselves to the whole range of ways in which we communicate.

Summarizing and Looking Ahead

No matter when, where, or how you communicate, you must understand the rules:

The more detailed ideas are, the more power they have.

The more senses are involved, the more power ideas have.

The more aligned your ideas are, the more cooperation you will experience—the more success you will enjoy together.

Success-Filing to expand exactly what you want to acknowledge: It's time to add more successes to your Success File. What holograms did you communicate in detail today? What details did you need to correct? What clarifying, detail-probing questions did you ask people you worked with? What inconsistencies did you notice and correct? When did you notice higher levels of cooperation because of well-communicated holograms?

In Skill 3 you were dreaming alone. In Skill 4 you were finding Codreamers. In Skill 5, with your dream well formed in your mind and your safety net in place, you will begin to search for people who will take action with you: Cooperators.

Since you live in a world that usually operates in First and Second Gears, you will begin confronting more people with reasons why your dream can't be realized. Some of those people will have more knowledge and experience than you do. Some will be certified and licensed and credentialed and even world-famous. Some of these experts' ideas will be far more detailed and powerful than yours.

What will happen when those huge holographic waves come rushing at you? Will you allow them to swamp you, or will you use them to empower you? Will they wash you ashore on some unfamiliar island wondering how you got there and what happened to your dream? What will happen if, in a desperate moment, you can't find your Codreamers?

The Best Codreamer of All Is Your Own Razz

Your own Razz is the part of the brain that compares the details of holograms you have in mind with the details of the sensory data coming in through your senses. It alerts you when there are similarities and opportunities. Your Razz is always there, keeping your dream safe, whether you realize it or not. Even your most loyal Codreamers won't always be there for you. They may be too busy, or you may not be able to reach them to reinstall your dream. Or your dream may have pressed them beyond their limits, taking them into parts of themselves they haven't explored—parts that gears and fears prevent them from entering, old rules and limits that they respect far more than your dream.

That's when you need to know that preliving your dream in your Razz is the ultimate fail-safe. Even when you've consciously given up on your dream, even when you've spent months trying to put it out of your mind, your Razz will continue alerting you to opportunities.

Not every idea comes at exactly the right time and place. Some ideas lie dormant for years. Charles Babbage, the father of the computer, conceived of an "analytical engine" in 1830. The materials he would need to build the precision gears and sprockets were not available in his time, so he completed detailed drawings of his "computer" to keep his dream alive. A hundred years later, a graduate student at Harvard stumbled upon his drawings and codreamed Babbage's 1830 idea into existence, changing our lives dramatically.

According to Victor Hugo, nothing is so powerful as an idea whose time has come. And an idea's time has come when a critical mass of people are also dreaming that idea: eliminating smallpox, sharing information worldwide, putting a man on the moon, discovering the origins of life in the universe, or extending and enjoying our lives here on Earth.

Skill 5

Using Others' Expertise

L ike a butterfly in a cocoon, you have been experiencing a slow, subtle metamorphosis. In First and Second Gears you were completing and deleting others' dreams—those of your parents, teachers, coaches, bosses, advertisers, and society. As you shifted into Third Gear, you began creating powerful dreams of your own and communicating them in detail as you searched for Codreamers. Having integrated their concerns and suggestions, you are ready to find people who will assist and challenge you far more. Now, instead of succeeding, you are moving into leadership—following your dream and leading others to journey with you.

Stepping Up to the Podium

A friend and I recently went to hear a performance of the New World Symphony. As we sat waiting for the concert to begin, glancing through our program and notes about the composers, the sound of each performer playing whatever he or she wanted became more and more strident. Finally, amid loud applause, the conductor stepped up to the podium and raised his baton powerfully, creating a oneness kept on course by his well-defined gestures and his players' constant upward glances. Together, they created something beyond what any one of those performers could have created alone. Together, they cocreated a concert that lived up to its name: Sacred and Sumptuous.

You are the composer and conductor of your own dream now. You will need to choose your players, hand out detailed scores, make corrections and changes, indicate timings and rhythms, and nod and gesture powerfully; this time *they* will be looking up to *you* as their leader. This may be an unfamiliar place for you at first. In fact you may feel more comfortable giving over that control to others who, you tell yourself, know more than you do, have longer résumés, and more years of experience. *But this time, instead of walking away at the end dissatisfied, you need to notice that you are stepping up on stage. You are picking up the baton. All those players are out there waiting for you to lead them. This time they are here to play your music—your way. And only you know which way that is.*

Not all the players you conduct will be creative performers operating in Third Gear. The conductor of our elementary school orchestra had to focus more time and energy on teaching us how to play on time than on making music. We were in First Gear, and he had to shift into First Gear with us. Even when we reached high school and were competently playing our parts, our personal agendas—competing for first chair and whispering about the weekend—were often more important than what our conductor was signaling. Oh, how our high school conductor must have longed to conduct an orchestra of talented, Third-Gear musicians who would be able to move beyond the notes to the music. But we weren't there yet and our conductors led us appropriately.

Where Can You Find Cooperators with the Expertise You Will Need?

In Skill 4 you were reaching out for Codreamers, people who would act as amplifiers and keepers of your dream. But now you are searching for people who have the time, energy, skills, and expertise you will need. You are searching for Cooperators, the group of people who will work with you to take your dream from a virtual to a time-and-space reality.

Sometimes the expertise you need will be delivered face-to-face. Sometimes it will arrive via systems created by experts: computers and software, Palm Pilots, voice-recognition technology, electronic security systems, mechanized watering systems, and computerized dating services. Before expert systems can become useful, you will need to learn how to use them. But will you slow down long enough to read their instructions? Will you invest the time needed to make expert systems useful and reliable to you and your Cooperators?

Today, instead of hiring experts, most of us start by purchasing a computer. Computers and computerized devices handle functions that people used to provide: bookkeeping, taxes, dictation, record keeping, filing, bill paying, information gathering, shopping, marketing, and mailing. But how will you decide which expert system you need? Who will you consult?

When we set out to find Codreamers, we sit down and chat, perhaps spending time over lunch or dinner or on the phone. But as soon as we reach out to someone who is willing and able to work with us, we are ready to bypass that step and jump right into action.

The Problem with Salespeople When You're in First Gear

Sometimes an urgent need sends us off to a store. The experts that greet us there are in Second Gear; their agenda is selling us products they're being paid to sell. After only cursory information taking, they make a diagnosis: "This is what you need." Perhaps there are other customers vying for attention; perhaps they believe they know what you need, but often they don't. The answer you get may not fit when you get home.

Striding into a nearby electronics store with my microcassette recorder in hand, I asked the salesman for a device that would slow down the playback so that I could transcribe tapes more easily. "No, we don't have that," he said quickly. But as I turned toward the door, he reached into a glass case and pulled out a digital recorder that, according to him, would transfer my spoken words into words on my computer screen. I was, to say the least, overjoyed. I could speak my notes and not have to transcribe them!

There was only one problem: This device and my computer couldn't communicate. To use it, I would have to journey from the Mac world I had known for years to the PC world. That was a shift I had planned to make soon to be compatible with my editor, but, with this added enticement, I decided to make it now. He showed me a computer with the Word software upgrade I wanted, a much larger monitor, and a combination fax/printer/scanner. Assured that after one hour I would be up and running even faster, I told him I would buy it all—if he had it all in stock. "No problem," he said.

No problem, that is, until I had my Ford Explorer parked on

the loading dock, back flipped down for what seemed like far too long. He finally emerged from the store to say, "Sorry, Susan, we don't have those components in stock after all. However, we will lend you a slightly smaller monitor and a one-step-down computer to use until your system arrives in five days. Then we will deliver your components, set them up, and make sure you are ready to go." Lacking the expertise to comprehend what setting up now and setting up again in five days would entail, and eager to get started, I nodded okay and he loaded three huge boxes into my car.

After unloading them, dragging them into my office, and pulling each component free from its vacuum-tight packing, I did have the new system *up and on* in about an hour. But I couldn't find the disk for Word, and its logo didn't appear on my screen either. When I called the store, they argued it was there. After a long hold, they told me the computer they'd lent me didn't come with Word, but if I would drive back over, they would give me a copy. I was beginning to melt down but rallied again, picked up the disk and installed it.

Finally the familiar terrain of Word appeared on my screen and I began exploring the upgraded expertise I had just purchased. With a tall stack of microcassettes sitting beside me, I decided to begin transcribing. Except for pushing that tiny rewind button over and over, it was pretty much straight typing. I was zooming ahead, thrilled as I watched words I almost typed correctly being corrected in front of my eyes, but as soon as I tried to save my work, I confronted an obstacle. When my left pinkie automatically reached for the control key, everything I had been typing for twenty minutes disappeared.

I couldn't figure out what I'd done wrong, but after starting again and losing another few minutes' work, I realized the control key was in a slightly different position. I would have to slow down until my brain and left hand could integrate this new arrangement. Okay, fine, I said to myself. I can handle this, too; it's all part of the process, and I continued to work, assuring myself that my days of transcribing were almost over . . . almost over. . . . *Almost over* was the mantra I chanted as I made my way through six hours of typing and finally went to bed.

I awoke early the next morning eager to see my new digital recorder/transcriber at work. Following the instructions, I practiced recording and playing back. At sunrise, instead of pocketing my old recorder, I took along my new one and digitally jotted down my notes, eagerly waiting for those words to appear magically, albeit technologically, on my screen. But having read and reread the instruction booklet and all the fine print, I couldn't figure out how to transcribe what I had recorded. Overwhelmed and disoriented, I put out a frantic call to a friend of mine who is a computer expert.

John had been urging me to make the switch into the PC world for years, so I knew I could count on him to bail me out now—even though I realized I had bypassed an essential step. I should have called him *before* I bought this system. When he arrived later, I felt foolish and said so. Before his crash-and-burn at age forty, John had been the bridge between man and computer all over Wall Street. Now I had what everyone in First Gear really wants: an expert beside me. Someone I had confidence in. Someone who had helped me with computer crises before. Someone who knew my needs and wasn't married to a particular product or brand. Someone who understood both the Mac and PC worlds. What would John do to get me back on track? John's first step was to shift me down all the way to stop.

Sensory Fill-In Is What You Want from Experts

Before John could cooperate, he needed as many multisensory details as I could provide, and wherever he sensed holes, he asked questions. John's in-depth analysis almost drove me mad, given the head of steam I had built up. But as nerve-racking as it was, I answered each of his questions as fully as possible. Before he could cooperate, he needed to codream with me.

Next John began matching my needs with the specifications of various product lines, and I wanted to argue that I had already done that completely, but I hadn't. Yes, for weeks I had been chatting with friends about which computer they used, noticing ads and hearing comments about whose tech support was best, but I was focused on writing. My only consolation was I could return any or all of what I had purchased. At that moment I felt quite inept, not because of John—who was neutral and supportive—but because of the conversation I was having with myself: "Why did I?" "How could I?" "Why didn't I?" But I was thrilled that John was here now and, instead of invalidating myself further, I began studying his approach.

The next day I felt affirmed when John called to say that, after analyzing my needs and making numerous calls, he felt the computer I had purchased would serve my needs well, and at a very good price with the rebates factored in. I took a deep breath, and my nerves settled down. But I wasn't prepared for the next words that came out of his mouth. "The digital recorder your salesman sold you won't do what he said. Yes, it will digitize your voice, but it was never designed to convert that recording to text. Sorry to say, Susan, the technological magic he described simply won't work." For the moment I was in shock—after buying a whole new computer and doing all this setup, after all these lost days. Then John told me it would take voice-recognition software to do what I had in mind, and he would have it shipped to me overnight. When I hung up I was so dazed and disoriented that—forget about creativity— the only thing I could do was go back to my transcribing, tiny rewind button and all.

When it comes to experts, Sensory Fill-In is a good thing. You want your experts to fill in methods you don't know and experience you don't have. You want them to fill in the multisensory details you can't fill in for yourself, making your dream far more powerful and possible. Next time, I needed to talk to my Fallback Expert first. What is a Fallback Expert? That's the person you plan to call when you can't figure something out, the person you silently count on to bail you out of problems in a particular area of expertise. How much expertise is available to you? Are you limited to the expertise of the salesman selling you the product? That salesman may have the best intentions and be the nicest person in the world, but he may be telling you what you can and can't do, what's possible and impossible based on his product line, his sales goal, or what his sales trainer incorrectly told him.

Training a Machine to Cooperate

The next morning the voice-recognition software arrived, and John called to say he would get started in the late afternoon. That was the day I was scheduled for the bone graft my dentist summarized as "You won't feel a thing." So based on what he said, I expected to be back in time to meet John, willing and able.

When I arrived, John was ready for me to begin training the software to recognize my voice. What a scene that was! There I sat, in front of my computer with a microphone around my neck and an ice pack on my jaw, reading children's stories to a machine. And yes, it was thrilling to finally see my spoken words popping up on my computer screen instantaneously and accurately! But when we geared up to the next level and I began reading it my own stories, what started popping up on the screen was 20 percent gibberish. I started to get scared. What if an important section of the book I was dictating came back looking like this? I wouldn't know what I said and I would have nothing to refer to.

Remember Sensory Fill-In. This software was doing exactly what people do when your instructions are unclear or they don't stop to ask. It was substituting words it knew for words it didn't recognize. In the interest of typing something, it was distorting what I said, like an answering machine playing back part of my message but making up the rest.

In my effort to do more-better-faster, I was being forced to slow down again, this time to teach the software the vocabulary I use. I could see that I would have to record, play back, and update over and over until we were finally speaking the same language. It would be months before this voice-recognition software would be useful and reliable, and since I would only be transcribing for a few months, I concluded it wasn't worth it. Success is also deletion!

A few minutes later, like a road-weary psychic, John lumbered in with a package under his arm. In an instant he opened it, plugged it in beside my desk, plopped in a microcassette, set down the foot control, and told me to get to work. What he had brought was exactly what I had set out to buy in the first place without knowing it—a Dictaphone. With a twinkle in his eye, John summarized, "In high-productivity, high-creativity situations, low-tech solutions are more useful because there is next to nothing to learn." And I heartily agreed as I began transcribing easily, keeping my typing speed in check but savoring the corrections my new computer was making. As confusing and disorienting as this last week had been, with John's expert guidance, I finally had what I needed: a low-tech method for transcribing notes and a high-tech computer system that was compatible with my editor's.

Virtual vs. Actual Staff

Yes, I was talking about training a machine, but you will have to go through the same process when you hire a new secretary, associate, designer, or sales rep. You can't suddenly gear back in a car—or in production—without stalling. John told me stories about companies that made equipment changes during production crises: instead of speeding things up, those changes slowed things down drastically, pushing people over the edge—the same edge I'd slipped over for a day or so. You have to plan ahead to shift into First Gear. Expecting people to learn under production pressure doesn't work. After that huge capital investment is made and all that sophisticated equipment is up and running, overwhelmed people will simply figure out how to do what they were doing already—but not more. They will operate within the limits of their old system instead of realizing the benefits of their new one.

The developers of my computer and the creators of its software are essential members of my team—unseen, unrecognized experts and coaches whom I rely on each day. I appreciate their instantaneous silent corrections and timely offers of help; I listen to their suggestions and respond to their warnings. The few thousand dollars I invested will yield far more support and expertise than I would have gotten by hiring a staff, without salaries, health insurance, workers' comp, extra desks, lights, phones, and all the other expenses involved in running an office—not to mention the time it would take to train and manage all those people. When I purchased this computer, I brought on board a whole team of experts I now have at my fingertips. And I have instantaneous 24/7 access to millions of as-yet-unmet experts worldwide.

Which Gear You're in Will Determine How You Approach Experts

Think about your phone list: Who are the people you call when you have a problem with your car, when your stocks go up or down, or when you want to plan your future? Whom do you call when you or a family member is not feeling well, when you have back pain or your pet is ill? Whom do you contact when an outlet isn't working, or when you want to redecorate or add another room? On the job, whose number do you dial when a computer glitch occurs, when you need help on a project, when a personnel issue is unclear, or when someone else's car is in your parking spot?

If you are in First Gear, with little or no knowledge and little or no experience, you will approach an expert or expert system in a childlike way; you need to be told exactly what to think and do, and you want him or her to take charge of your method and even the details of your dream. Yes, by all means use experts but *stay alert.* When you are in First Gear, you are most likely to be overwhelmed by others' highly detailed holograms and experience; you are most likely to get what *they* want instead of what *you* want. Choose your experts carefully. And remember, no matter how much they know or how much experience they have, you are still responsible for leading them to *your* dream.

If you are in Second Gear, you are effective and efficient in this skill area as well, and there will be a tendency to compete with your experts: "But I think you should . . ." or "This approach would work better." Second-Gear Cooperators—electricians, carpenters, painters, roofers, sales, and production people—lease themselves on an hourly or a commission basis. So for them time is money; they are constantly pressing against deadlines and having to choose between quantity and quality. You will need to make sure your job is done completely before time and money pull them ahead to their next customer. If you are in Third Gear, you will be eager to collaborate about the details of your hologram, preliving the whole process. You need to check in with your expert on a regular basis to make sure you are still aligned, and to take responsibility for any unaligned Sensory Fill-In that occurs in your absence.

Most people operate in one or two gears, but some operate in all three. Effective, competitive, creative leaders like John—travel agents, meeting planners, designers, architects, contractors, project managers, and consultants of various kinds—help you flesh out exactly what you want and manage its implementation. Not simply

focused on what's right and possible, or how to do it most efficiently, they are committed to helping you complete *your* dream,
whatever it is, regardless of how unusual or individual it is.

He said, she said, but which expert is right? Whose advice
should you follow? Not all experts agree, and at times you will find
yourself trying to sort through conflicting advice. Here's a suggestion. Take a look at which gear those conflicting experts are using.
Experts like John, who use all three gears, are most appropriate
when you start. *The less you know, the more you will need your expert to
know. The more you know, the less you will need your expert to know.*

Pick Your First Cooperator Carefully

As you begin to look for support and expertise, make sure that
the first person you bring on board is in detailed multisensory alignment with you. Choose him or her carefully, because
that person may be the one who will carry your dream to the next
person, who will carry it to the next person, and so on, as in the old
game of telephone. Make sure you record–play back–update with
that first person over and over, because if he or she is clear, that
clarity will circulate throughout your whole organization.

With his expert systems in place, Carlos was generating so
much real-estate business that he couldn't keep up despite his
high-tech "virtual staff," and there was finally enough income to
hire his first associate. But what exactly did he want this person to
do? And how would he recognize him or her in a résumé or an
interview? Carlos was searching for someone who was willing and
able to codream and cooperate in growing his business, someone
who was flexible and creative and could use the systems he had in
place. After interviewing for weeks, he met a young woman whose
skills, background, and future plans aligned with his dream. They
had an easy rapport, and part-time work was fine for her to start.

Looking ahead to the next quarter, Carlos listed the jobs he expected. Which parts of these jobs did he want her to handle: follow-up, follow-through, letters, calls, and prospecting? As he listed each task, I pressed him to go deeper. Exactly what would his new associate need to know before she could write a letter, or handle a client call, or access a file? What would Carlos need to do to get her ready to assist him? And what would he have to do to give her the Big Picture of his industry and how his firm fit in it? His new associate may already know how to do the tasks Carlos wants her to assume, but if she doesn't have his business clearly in mind, if she doesn't know his clients and how to quickly locate their files and the data within them, if she doesn't feel confident about asking questions, if she isn't already accelerating along in Second Gear, then when he hands the baton to her, she won't be able to keep pace with him. But if she is in sync, then she will be able to run along beside him and sometimes pull ahead.

What creates alignment? Up-front analysis that seems like paralysis; answering questions you want to swat at like flies: "No, I don't have time. . . . Not now, I've got a deadline, conference call, or meeting. . . ." Soon that new employee, who is still waiting two weeks later for your reply, hates your guts. The customer who was told "It'll only take an hour to be up and running faster than ever," who is sitting in her office in a sweat before calling in other experts, is the very person who complains to your customer service reps. The questions you don't want to hear or set aside time to answer up front are the very questions you need to answer to create alignment and cooperation, to make experts and expert systems useful and reliable.

Share Your Whole Dream with Your Team

Another common mistake we make when we hire new people is giving them only part of the picture. If you give them only one piece, the piece you think they need, then they won't be able to figure out how that piece fits, because they have never seen the picture on top of the puzzle box. As a result, they will be unable to cross-reference, cross-train, cross-function, or cocreate. Either they will keep coming back to you for a decision, or they will decide on their own. And if they choose the latter, chances are good that you will be called on to solve an even bigger problem down the road. Giving your new hires only part of the picture may seem expedient at the moment, but it reduces the competence and creativity they can bring to you and your team in the long run. This approach may work fine with a temp worker but not with someone you plan to cooperate with over time.

Highly successful people in successful organizations have told me many times that they often don't know who will create the idea that will take their project or dream to the next level . . . and the person is not necessarily someone they think of as creative. It could be anyone who has the whole dream in mind, anyone who has had an experience that might be relevant or who knows somebody who has had such an experience. Therefore, you need to communicate your dream to Cooperators in as much detail as possible. Only you know *exactly* what your dream looks, sounds, and feels like. Only you know the rights and wrongs of your dream, the have-tos and musts. And one of those musts must be "It's possible!"

When those who come to cooperate start looking at your dream, talking it over, and discovering how it feels to them, they will begin adding details of their own, altering and adjusting, reshaping and remolding your dream. Then, like a parent supervising a nanny, you will be in charge of maintaining your dream's safety and integrity. Other dreams may interfere; familiar ways of thinking may become more important; old methods may seem more appropriate. At some point, you may need to release a player from your team. No matter what, you are responsible for keeping your dream alive and on course, for eliminating distractions, diversions, and oppositions; at the same time, you are responsible for including the contributions others make to your dream and negotiating that fine line. This expanded leadership role may not be comfortable at first. Suddenly your dream seems unreal again; suddenly their questions hit blind spots and leave you inwardly staggering. "How could I have overlooked that? Thank goodness they asked me! I wonder what else I haven't thought through all the way."

What You Couldn't See from the Success Side

When you started learning, you depended on your leaders to tell you exactly what, when, and how, the way John did as he stood beside me and my computer for a few days. When you were struggling to become productive, you depended on your leaders to remain available, measure your results, and assess when, in their view, you were ready for increases in responsibility and compensation.

You weren't able to see from the success side that what allowed them to lead you was a dream: a dream they were holding clearly in mind, a dream they had altered and adjusted thousands of times and become skillful at sharing; they were committed to living this dream no matter what. And what you couldn't see from the success side was that included in the dream was a vision of passing it on so that you could participate: Your questions would expand your understanding and theirs; your shortcuts and adjustments would make the whole process more efficient; your ahas, realizations, and intuitions would make their dream your dream, allowing you to step up into leadership, too.

Why are so many people stressed, unhappy, unfulfilled, and uncertain about what to do and when to do it? Because the success process went awry when leaders failed to pass on the dream. In the interest of time or one-upmanship, they told you to "do this" or "do that," but they didn't tell you how or why. You had to keep asking, pestering, even begging. With only one piece of an unknown puzzle in hand, you were forced to either remain dependent, not knowing where your piece fit and therefore afraid to make decisions or take timely steps, or to start making up answers and heading in your own direction, one that became more misaligned day by day, conflicting with what your boss secretly had in mind. There were clashes and arguments but no real exchange of the needed Big Picture. Maybe you kept working at that job because you had credit cards, mortgages, and other dreams—buying a new car or larger home, sending your kids to college, contributing to your retirement, or taking a family vacation—so you became stagnated and bored, jaded and rebellious, disillusioned and ambivalent, stressed and ill. Maybe the only reason you stayed was the money.

But now, in Third Gear, it's your own dream you're creating. Finally you are the composer and conductor of your dream. Whether it's writing a book, building your career, creating a start-up, decorating your home, or leading your family, you need to choose each of your players carefully, hand out detailed scores, indicate appropriate timings and rhythms, make outcome-oriented corrections and changes. This time you are the one they will be looking to for guidance. This time you will be the one who needs to step up and lead!

Old Notions About Leadership
Take You to the Breaking Point

Y*ou will begin to realize that the leaders you have been seeking certainty from have been dealing with uncertainty, too. The closer you get to your dream, the less black-and-white it seems; the more soft and fluid and vaporous and changing it grows; the more obvious it becomes that what lies behind each dream is a thought or a hologram.*

But here's the rub: What your First- and Second-Gear Cooperators most need is a black-and-white plan—right/wrong, good/bad. What your Second-Gear Cooperators most want to know is which methods, systems, equipment, charts, graphs, positions, titles, promotions, and bonuses you will use—a level of certainty you may simply not have at this point in the process. That's why you need to bring on experts who can operate in all three gears, those who know they must codream with you before they can devise effective plans, develop efficient methods, and break through to creative solutions. These are experts you know you can fall back on.

Leaders, like succeeders, struggle with uncertainty and not knowing. They find themselves pressed against their First-Gear expectation that they should know how to do everything right. They feel the accelerating pressures of their Second-Gear expectation that they should be able to do everything better than anyone else. With these ideas driving them, they work harder and harder to appear definite and certain; they struggle to articulate long-term plans when they really don't know what's happening; they posture to convey clarity and certainty for boards and investors and press themselves and their teams unmercifully to make those projections come true. Remember how Tom's boss tried to cover up his pain by partying? Remember how those First-Gear policemen put him in jail to protect his health and well-being and that of others on the highways, leaving the whole mess in Tom's lap?

Think about leaders you have had who were less than supportive. You may find yourself feeling more empathetic and understanding of their deficiencies now that you are walking in their shoes. It is remarkable how brilliant our parents suddenly look when we arrive home from the hospital with a new baby. And it is also remarkable how much compassion you will begin to feel for bosses who were too pressed to communicate or too uncertain and unsure themselves to give you all the details you needed, once you become one. What they did may not have worked, but it is understandable. For better or worse, your past leaders will be the examples your Razz refers to as you begin leading. Unless you have a clearly defined hologram of the kind of leader you want to be, you will find yourself automatically and unconsciously doing what they did. Remember, what you think is what you get, like or it not.

You Don't Have to Be Able to Do It to Lead It

At this point in the success and leadership process, we come to realize that what makes people highly successful isn't what they know or can do; it's their commitment to a well-formed dream and their ability to attract support and expertise. John F. Kennedy didn't know how to put a man on the moon, but he did know that if he communicated his vision in enough detail to enough people and generated enough power and enthusiasm, the scientists, inventors, manufacturers, and citizens of our nation would rise to the occasion and provide the materials, expertise, and money he needed. In response to Kennedy's powerful media-communicated dream, we got excited as a nation; we were eager to hear each tiny bit of news, each success story, week after week, month after month, year after year. And, wherever we were, we were glued to our TV sets as the first man from Earth stepped onto that unfamiliar lunar surface. And the fulfillment of this enormous, unprecedented dream inspired the next generation of space explorers and success explorers on our planet to communicate and fulfill their own dreams.

Third-Gear leaders have the ability to guide others to their dream; they can communicate a clear hologram; they are able to find or develop necessary skills; they can inspire others to keep going even in moments when every fiber of their being screams *Quit!* They can get that potential champion up one more time—the very time she or he will outperform everyone else in the world and earn the Gold Medal; the very time a child is finally able to climb all the way to the top of a rope; the very time a teenager is finally able to parallel-park, pass an exam, get a job, meet a quota, or say no to something that takes him or her off course.

Third-Gear leaders are wise enough to allow others to lead them. Instead of feeling threatened or wrong or overpowered or competed with, they simply continue detailing and refining and integrating the expertise, information, and feedback coming in until they finally know for certain they have arrived. They feel complete.

Then, instead of taking the credit, as Second-Gear succeeders would, they have the wisdom to acknowledge everyone who helped them along the way, realizing that this is a Third-Gear success, one enjoyed because of others' expertise. Third Gear is about sharing and respecting expertise, not going back to school to learn how to do it all yourself. Third Gear is about knowing that a beautiful home you codreamed and cooperated with others to complete is your dream enjoyed. Third Gear is about knowing that the success you and your organization produce is a success for each and every one of you. In Third Gear, success is a shared experience. Whether you are celebrating the success produced for you by a skilled painter or carpenter, a skilled and dedicated sales manager or production manager, a skilled day care worker or teacher, in Third Gear those successes are all yours as well—your successes as a leader.

Learning as You Lead, Leading as You Learn

Leadership is a learning process. Make sure you set aside time to discover what you and your team are learning. What questions do they have about your shared dream? What details have *they* changed slightly that *you* need to change, too? What feedback have they gotten that you need to know and use as well? Whether you make it all the way to completion or not, whether you are pulling together or apart will depend on how well the multisensory details of your holograms match—whether the person you are leading is selling your product, solving problems for your customers, mowing your lawn, decorating your home, or, most important of all, taking care of your children. Whether you are cooperating in the same room or a million miles apart, you will all need to build the same hologram in as much detail as possible. Your Razzes must search for the same things.

I was excited to be able to teach *The Technology of Success* to the CNN Financial News (CNNfn) team. Lou Dobbs is a talented and experienced newscaster, but he didn't have the expertise to bring a network to life all alone. By detailing and amplifying their dream together day by day, week by week, he and his Codreamers were able to attract a powerful team. But a team that had never brought a TV network into existence either.

Together they let their dream lead them; together they were willing to be energized by dilemmas and ahas, to discuss, argue, and align on new details and next steps. Together they were willing to respond to the feedback that came in, to ask experts what they needed to know, to learn what they needed to do, and to shift gears up and down each time they needed to change their method and approach. Together they pressed themselves against deadlines and through exhaustion until finally, on that prelived day, they stood there waiting to see their CNNfn programming pop up on TV screens around the room. And when that moment arrived, they let out a huge cheer, hugged, high-fived, and enjoyed their dream—realized and acknowledged together.

I remember sitting with that team a year later, laughing about how scary it had been for them to proclaim they would get CNNfn on the air by a specific time and date, to advertise that fact and collect advertisers' monies based on it. We chuckled over all the butterflies and uncertainties they had experienced as that deadline approached, all the snafus and foul-ups and phone calls and mad dashes and last-minute crises and corrections. Thanks to his team, Lou became the face of television financial news around the world. It was quite an achievement for a young group of techies with a bulldog-dreamer at their head.

But the original team usually doesn't run the whole race. As the dream progresses, like the next runner in a relay, new team members take over. I have seen numerous start-up teams launch projects. They thrive on the challenge of finding the right people and inspiring them to get the dream moving. But they aren't necessarily the best people to move into the productivity and competition phases. In fact, at CNNfn, when the adrenaline rush of getting the network up and running and building its ratings and reputation subsided, another crew—one skilled at Second-Gear production and quality-system development and the Third-Gear ability to keep it growing and changing and responding to the crop of new competitors—stepped in. Finally, like most good new ideas, the financial news was absorbed into CNN's day-to-day programming.

Moving Past Your Fear of Experts

We all need expertise, but sometimes we don't reach for it because, based on past experience, we are afraid that asking an expert will limit our options or, worse, prevent us from pursuing our dream. In truth, some experts are authorized to prevent us from obtaining a license and practicing a skill—driving, selling, healing, building, manufacturing, or distributing—without sufficient expertise or sufficient supervision, but they are not empowered to prevent us from finding experts to assist us.

Sometimes we fail to get the expertise we need because we're afraid it will cost too much or take too much time. Besides, we know that some competitive experts will try to convince us that their ideas are better than ours and we're afraid we'll cave in. We've caved in in the past, when their thoughts were so multisensory and detailed, so magnetic and attractive, that without even realizing it, we were more attracted to their holograms than our own, and we regretted it later. And, yes, we need to realize that in Second Gear there is a contest going on between what we think and they think, what we want and what they want.

But in Third Gear, you rise above these fears, knowing everything you see, hear, and feel an expert doing is simply another cluster of details you can add to your dream to make it more powerful and possible. You begin to recognize that when it comes to your dream you are the only person in the world who knows or can discover exactly what you want. You are the ultimate expert and, to stay true to your dream, you must step up *now*. After a while you may not remember whose idea it was or how you got it, it will just be yours to use and pass on.

We usually think we move into leadership when we're given a title or position at work or are elected to an office in a civic organization. Leadership is something we unconsciously expect other people to give us. But the truth is, you must choose to lead whenever you choose to use someone else's expertise to support you.

If you fail to lead, you won't get what you want. Yes, you'll get that outlet installed in the living room but not where you want it. You'll get everyone to sit down together for a meeting but not handle the agenda item that matters most to you. You will pay someone to redecorate your house, but it may never feel like home. You won't get what you want, not because of them, but because you let your experts lead you to *their* dream instead of your own. Yes, they may know a heck of a lot about a heck of a lot of things, but when it comes to your dream, they simply won't know—unless you lead them.

Success-Filing expertise: What successes have you had because you asked an "expert" for help: a friend who knew more about something than you did, a teacher or coach, a salesman or customer service rep? Did you ask on the phone or in person? Were you able to ask for assistance even though you were uncomfortable? When did you stop to read a manual or instruction sheet even though you would have preferred to muddle through on your own? When did you provide expertise to others? When did you slow down enough to answer First-Gear questions? When did you share expertise that might have put someone else's production ahead of yours? When did you make suggestions that took someone else's idea to the next level? When did you share your expertise with your team?

Beyond Words, Beyond Notes, Beyond Individuals

During the Sacred and Sumptuous concert, all the players could have been soloists. They all had the skill; they all had the experience. When those players chose to become part of the orchestra, they committed to doing whatever was needed in each performance. They committed to aligning 100 percent of their skill and musicality with what their conductor was signaling. Even though they were not the composer, the conductor, or soloists, the extraordinary quality of their shared performance gave them a joy that transcended individual performance.

Beyond words, beyond notes, beyond scores, beyond plans—this kind of synergistic alignment occurs whenever people are truly codreaming and cooperating. Miracles happen; wondrous serendipities occur that move your performance beyond anything you had previously achieved or anticipated. Actors regularly speak of those moments when something else happens, when the character takes over. In those moments, expertise—information and experience gained in First and Second Gears—is far surpassed as the performance moves into creativity, spontaneity, and inspiration. The type of performance doesn't matter: a ballet, a symphony, a football game, a high-powered corporate board meeting, or a space shot. The audience, as one mesmerized body, springs to its feet as soon as the performance is over. There is ecstasy and triumph that goes beyond anything else we know as human beings.

Updating Your Past

My daughter Margaret had been fantasizing about having a rose garden for years. Finally she and her husband Steve moved into their own home and, for her next birthday, instead of cut roses he gave her "a rose garden" built to her dream specifications and installed by an expert. Margaret was in tears.

When her gardener arrived, one of the first questions he asked Margaret was where. Together they picked a sunny spot where family and friends would pass whenever they came in and out of their home, a spot where rose-loving neighbors would enjoy passing as well. But it was also a spot where grass and hedges that were thriving everywhere else wouldn't grow. Why?

Her gardener pushed down with his boot to lift out a shovel full of soil. The blade slid easily through the first few inches but then struck something solid. After multiple tries, her gardener discovered that six inches beneath the surface of their lawn lay an old driveway that had been sodded over years ago. That's why the grass burned out in the summer. That's why hedges wouldn't grow, and why her roses wouldn't grow either unless they punched holes around each plant. With that old driveway still intact, no matter how much watering she did, no matter how many sprays, fertilizers, or special foods she applied, Margaret's roses wouldn't bloom.

Each of us has "old driveways" beneath the surface of our lives. Perhaps we don't realize they're there. Maybe we don't remember when they were laid down or who put them there, but we know something is stopping us. Dreams we try to grow simply don't flourish—no matter how much confidence we build, no matter how many Success Gears we shift, no matter how detailed our dreams are, or how well we communicate them. And no matter how many experts we call.

Success Is Deletion: Releasing the Brakes

Success is completion, and it's also deletion—the deletion of old rules and limits you were taught to use or decided you needed to use earlier in your life. Are those rules and limits still useful now? Or are they getting in your way? In Skills 3, 4, and 5, you learned how to create highly detailed, multisensory dreams and share them with others. But to reach those dreams, you will also have to learn how to update the highly detailed, multisensory memories that have been holding you back all these years—limits that up until now have been far more attractive than living your dreams!

What upsets are you experiencing because First- and Second-Gear holograms still lie intact beneath the surface of your life? How much time and energy are you losing each day because you are still automatically and unconsciously attempting to complete them? In Skill 6 you will learn how to release your brakes and assist others in releasing theirs as well.

In the next few pages, the prefix *re* will appear over and over. *Re* means *again*, to go back to a previous state or condition. Skill 6 is about *re*—*re*viewing, *re*hearing, *re*feeling, *re*thinking, *re*including, *re*deciding, *re*leasing, *re*dreaming, *re*discovering, and *re*committing. In Skill 3 you *pre*experience your future in order to lay down new holograms for your brain to reference. In Skill 6 you *re*experience your past—consciously using today's level of information, knowledge, and expertise to give it a more up-to-date meaning.

Brothers-in-Law Who Couldn't Find Each Other in the Same Time and Space

Where are your "old driveways" most likely to be? In areas you avoid, areas you fear, areas you've failed at repeatedly or failed to try at all, areas where other people upset you. Here's an example of two people who thought they were operating on the surface of their lives but who had actually slipped underground into old times and spaces.

Chuck and Dan found themselves in a shouting match on the phone. Initially they were supporting their wives through an upset, but within seconds Chuck and Dan lost their present-time orientation and plunged deep into past pain: Dan into avoiding the fear he felt during his parents' financial ups and downs; Chuck into attempting to protect his life after his father died and his older brother fell to his death a few years later. Once that fateful door to the past had been reopened and its contents rushed forth, it was hard for them to find their way back to the present and to retract words said, and meant, in that confused state.

Who were they really yelling at in that moment? Each other? Or their fathers or brothers? Was it God or fate? Their Razzes automatically and unconsciously took over in that moment. This looks like . . . This sounds like . . . This feels like . . . Old wounds were reopened, old pain reactivated, old behaviors reenacted. Months later they were still struggling to reconnect in the present.

Chuck was still using his "think everything through before you do anything" approach that he had decided would keep him safe after the deaths of his father and brother. He didn't want to say anything until he'd had a chance to cool down and think. He was busy getting ready for vacation; then he'd be out of town—so it seemed *reasonable* to him to wait until he got back to call Dan.

But after three weeks—even though Chuck finally said all the right things—Dan didn't feel his apology was sincere. He felt Chuck had only apologized because Thanksgiving was coming, and mothers, mothers-in-law, wives, and kids wanted to sit down to dinner together. Without an apology he could accept, Dan refused the dinner invitation. His long-ago-decided approach to upsets was to wall them off and ignore them, so he never even considered the possibility that Chuck's words—offered in his own time—were sincere. Dan's place at the Thanksgiving table was empty that year, and both their kids couldn't understand why. Or why, when their dads finally got together at the next family gathering, they shook hands.

Close the Door to the Past Quickly

Chuck apologized, but he didn't apologize the moment he heard the offending words come out of his mouth or call back an hour later or even the next day. When we have upsets, we need to make completing them a priority, because the more time that passes, the more feelings slip through that open door to the past. The more time passes, the more Sensory Fill-In is added, and the more layered, detailed, and multisensory that upset becomes.

Even though Chuck wasn't ready to talk, he could have E-mailed or left messages—something as simple as "Dan, I'm sorry," or something as real as "I don't know what happened, I overreacted. I'd like to talk when we come back from vacation." And even though Dan preferred a faster response, he needed to stay open to the sincerity of someone else's timing and approach.

In Third Gear, we realize upsets in the present are seeded by similar upsets in the past—all the times our mothers, fathers, sisters, brothers, teachers, bosses, or friends did or didn't do this or that. Old upsets are setups for upsets in the moment. Let me say that again: Old upsets are setups for upsets in the moment. Whenever we're incomplete, our Razz automatically and unconsciously sorts for similar situations in our past. Then suddenly, instead of simply dealing with the current upset, we are dealing with all the upsets we've ever had.

Time heals, or does it? After all this time, why are some old situations still so highly charged? Because we recharge them each time we remember them *from the same perspective.* In Skill 6, we will look at those situations again from a Third-Gear perspective— unlocking those experiences and releasing energies that have been tied up and unavailable for years.

Highly Successful People Update the Past as Well as the Future

Highly successful people change their minds about the future as well as the past. They regularly take time to venture back into old scenes, updating the version of memory they have stored there. Instead of continuing to use the 2.0 version, or the 5.0, 18.5, 25.0, they update old memories based on what they know and do now.

We live in a media world of ads and commercials; computers, digital editing, and graphic enhancement; body-resonating sound systems, big-screen TVs, and ever-larger movie screens. When we dig down below the surface, we see that technology is allowing other people to do *for us* or *to us* what we are capable of doing *for ourselves*—that is, changing our minds—by adjusting pictures and sound tracks, changing actors and how they play their parts, and rewriting scripts, thereby altering our feelings and actions.

Remember, to the brain, recorded past memories (holograms) and created future memories (holograms) are the same. You can update incomplete scenes virtually or holographically, laying down "successful memories" you can access from now on.

What Is Updating?
Reexperiencing and Redeciding

Updating is reexperiencing times in your past when you were incomplete—when you failed to do what you set out to do; when parents, caregivers, relatives, friends, teachers, coaches, or bosses let you down; or when life dealt you an unexpected blow. But this time, instead of looking at those scenes from your old fixed-camera position—the way you've *always* seen them—you will reexperience them from as many angles as possible.

In Third Gear you have a choice: You can leave your old holographic memories in place as you originally recorded them and continue unconsciously re-creating and reenacting those scenes in an unconscious attempt to complete them. Or you can revisit those old scenes consciously and complete them for yourself now.

A Bump in the Road:
Reuniting Friends

Marianne and Carol were best friends growing up in New Jersey. Their houses were so close that they could whisper out the window after they'd been told to go to bed. They were in the same ballet class and the same class in school; they had the same friends— until years later, when in one searing moment their lives were torn apart.

Carol's brother died tragically, and Carol reached out to her best friend, who was now living in Florida, but Marianne had an infant with an ear infection and he wasn't well enough to fly. Even if there had been someone to look after her baby, she wouldn't have felt right about leaving him home sick.

The choices they made in that moment were no longer the same. Based on their childhood, Carol felt that Marianne should have flown to New Jersey to be with her, no matter what. And Marianne felt her best friend should have understood that taking care of her sick child had to take precedence. Marianne did everything she could do, short of going there.

Because of the excruciating tearing apart they experienced, they hadn't spoken for years. Precious moments were flying by; their children were in the same stage of life Carol and Marianne had enjoyed as best friends. Hoping to share their lives and families again, they reached past the pain by phone and by letter and planned a reunion midway between their homes.

Even though they couldn't finalize their plans because Marianne's husband's schedule would not be known until closer to the reunion weekend, to solidify their intention, they made a hotel reservation they knew they could cancel if he couldn't take care of the kids. But as the weekend grew near, another priority came up for Marianne, an event she had tentatively said yes to a year before, and she E-mailed Carol that the date was in question. And the upset was reactivated. Carol felt Marianne wasn't making her a priority *again,* not because of her husband's schedule, but because of something another friend had invited her to do that Marianne had never mentioned.

In the spirit of Carol's current level of growth, she E-mailed Marianne to express her feelings, but when Marianne read her E-mail she heard it as yelling. She heard the same anger and tragic disappointment she'd heard in Carol's voice all those years before, and instead of being excited about their upcoming weekend she was scared that they would wind up in a hotel room in an unfamiliar city hopelessly mired down in old pain.

Reactivated: Sometimes the Child Within Us Takes Over Again

What had caused all that pain? Carol's father had left home when Carol was a girl, abandoning her need for his love and support. Meanwhile, next door, Marianne's father yelled and screamed so violently and threateningly that her mother divorced him. With those earlier, similar incompletions rushing through the open door to the past, Carol was *re*acting to being abandoned. And Marianne was *re*acting to being yelled at until her family fell apart. But like ripples from raindrops, those old waves of pain had radiated out so far from their source that it was no longer obvious where they were coming from. And instead of looking to the past, Carol and Marianne were looking for the source of their pain in each other, here and now.

Upsets between adults are deceptive: That cardiologist or executive you are consulting, that chart-topping salesperson or Wall Street whiz you are strategizing with suddenly becomes the hurt child yelling at you. *How can you recognize when the inner child takes over? Listen for the cues: right/wrong, good/bad, can/can't, always/never, have to/must, possible/impossible, and, most of all, urgent need and disproportionate upset.*

Update: Now We Are the Caregiving, Protective Adults

To shift into Third Gear, we must recognize a very important fact: As young children we had every right to expect to come first. Our cries, hungers, and requests needed to be responded to as close to immediately as possible. Meeting our needs and wants was our parents' most sacred responsibility. We were immature and unskilled. We needed our parents and caregivers to be our protectors, confidence-builders, teachers, communicators, Codreamers, Cooperators, and experts of all kinds. We needed them to be able to use all the Success Skills you have learned so far.

In those areas where our parents and caregivers met our needs and wants, we have moved ahead easily. But in those areas where they were unable or unwilling to meet our needs—in a timeless, holographic universe—we still expect those needs to be met.

But we are not babes in the crib anymore, and now we are trying to get those needs met by people who do not have that sacred responsibility; people who are not charged with our care and protection and who are relating to the part of us they see in front of them—our adult part.

Today we must learn to take care of our own frustrated inner child and to let him or her know that we are the caregiving, protective adults now. We have been there and done that, and we know how it feels. This time our inner child can relax. This time—with these Success Skills in mind—we will make sure his or her incomplete needs are met lovingly, skillfully, and completely. We are stepping up to leadership in our own lives.

Finding Yourself on the Holodeck

When you find yourself upset, stop to consider the possibility that the person in front of you is playing out a different scene in a different time and place, that somehow—as in Star Trek—you have stepped up onto the Holodeck and entered another reality. You have suddenly been transported into the body of a father who screamed and yelled until your friend's family fell apart into one who, in overwhelming upset, abandoned your best friend as a girl. Or you are unexpectedly playing your brother-in-law's father, who forced him to deal with financial uncertainties he didn't know how to handle; or you have unknowingly become a father who died before he'd had a chance to teach his son how to handle upsets and offer timely apologies.

And stop to consider the possibility that you may have been transported back into your own past, into a younger part of you. You are somewhere else, expecting him or her to know where you are and what you need without explanation, without even knowing that this reality shift has taken place.

Will you realize who you are, and where you are, quickly enough to respond appropriately? Or will you assume that all upset is directed at you? Will you take it personally instead of holographically?

What Kind of Relationship Do You Want Now?

Once Marianne's childhood reaction subsided and she stepped into present time, she recognized the validity of what Carol had said. And with both her kids well and well cared for, she wholeheartedly agreed that their reunion was her highest priority.

Next Marianne and Carol needed to update their relationship. What kind of relationship did they want *now* that they were mothers living in different states? Would they talk every day the way they had when living next door, sharing dreams and challenges, upsets and hard decisions—this time by E-mail or phone? Would they spend family holidays and vacations together or simply get away for an occasional weekend?

And how would they reunite? Where in the airport would they each be waiting? Where would they go? Would they be polite and scripted, or would they open themselves up to what would happen?

What Can You Learn from Highly Successful Actors?

What do actors have to do to get beyond their personalities and previous performances? When Meryl Streep was in her first acting class at Vassar, as she stepped on the stage she stepped into another reality. Suddenly she was a famous actress at the end of her career thanking the people who had been there for her. Tears filled her eyes as she thanked those who had inspired and cheered her on, who selected her for parts she didn't know she could play: parts that forced her to stretch beyond her usual limits, unfamiliar parts that pressed her to see life from new angles, say things she would normally never say, feel things she would normally protect herself from feeling, do things that were out of character for her. She was grateful to the people in her audiences who allowed her to be far more of who she was. And gratified that the Academy had given her Awards for doing that.

Meryl said her friends in the audience were shocked. The Meryl they saw up there wasn't the one they knew. No, in that moment, she had created a detailed, multisensory hologram and stepped into it so convincingly that she and her audience were moved to tears—so convincingly that she spent the rest of her life living it. So too, in an update, we must go beyond our old scripts and approaches. We must know what we want to achieve in that scene but be flexible and responsive to nuances.

When Academy Award–winner Christopher Walken was a student at the Actor's Studio, he was playing his part, as written, when a huge platter of dishes suddenly smashed in the back of the theater. Maintaining his scripted approach, he continued delivering his lines as if nothing had happened. Studio head Lee Strasberg stopped him abruptly. He told Walken that his audience heard those dishes smash and that he needed to communicate that he heard them, too, instead of trying to pretend that nothing had happened.

Their Reunion: Stepping on Stage

As Marianne and Carol walked off their planes and headed into the airport, they stepped into the reality of being best friends—not childhood but adult friends. They each brought presents wrapped in beautiful papers and ribbons. Each carried pictures of her spouse and kids. Catching sight of each other in the agreed-upon spot and noticing the changes those years had brought, they rushed into each other's arms the way they had longed to for years. Over coffees, lunches, and dinners they chatted endlessly in a mad dash to catch up, to fill in those missing years.

Once they were home, their friendship continued as though never interrupted; they called to share whenever their kids won soccer games or came down with fevers; they E-mailed each other to strategize and affirm, to leap up into metaphysical realms they had never shared before.

When Carol visited her old neighborhood months later and drove by their houses still sitting there side by side, instead of feeling disconnected and disappointed the way she had last time, she was grateful that she and Marianne had grown up together and their families would, too—now that they'd moved beyond a bump in the road.

Disorienting: Letting Go of Your Old Point of View

To lead others to your dream, you will have to lead yourself back through the pathways and alleyways of your past into places where leaders let you down, places you decided you would *never* go again—*never* relook at, relisten to, refeel, or redo—places you have resisted or avoided ever since. But those old decisions may not be working now and some of those avoided behaviors may be essential to achieving your dream.

Remember the ancient mazes described in Skill 1 and the reason healers sent people through them? Yes, it was to disorient them. To assist them in letting go of their stuck thinking so that they could think and behave in a different way and make the changes needed for health and well-being, happy relationships and families, and successful approaches. Even though one of those taller-than-a-man mazes can't be found in your neighborhood, you will be able to let go of your old pains and decisions using the Success Skills you are learning.

What is it that you have refused to look at in your past? What have you been unwilling to rehear and reconsider, refeel and redecide? Given what you know now, those old experiences will look, sound, and feel different. And you will be able to decide differently about them, too, changing not only your reaction to your past but also to your future, thereby reopening possibilities you closed years ago.

In First Gear We Need Leaders to Protect Us— and to Teach Us to Protect Ourselves

In the Washington political arena, a world of sex, power, and abuse, Sharon was a powerhouse. She could get bills on the legislative docket and past roadblocks as effectively as anyone there. She was the person people came to for support, strategies, and insights. She knew how to deal with difficult people and situations.

Her job was her life; she worked until eight or nine and spent weekends catching up with the enormous workload she kept shouldering. No matter how supportive Sharon was of her boss and organization, they weren't supportive of her. And when she did manage to pull herself away from her desk, she spent her off-hours with "friends" and "boyfriends" others could clearly see were "users" and "abusers." Exhausted and disappointed, she found her way to my office.

Behind her beautiful smile, Sharon was suffering the same pain she had suffered at home as a child. Sharon's mother was afraid of her husband's constant sexual demands. She numbed herself with alcohol and tried reaching outside her marriage for the love and attention she needed. Even when her husband became enraged and abusive, she still stayed—too many kids, too little money, too many responsibilities to leave.

At four, instead of being protected by her mother, Sharon became her mother's protector. Sharon tried to do everything she could to make her mom's life easier. And when her father started approaching four-year-old Sharon sexually, she remained silent—violated, in pain, desperate—not wanting to create any more problems for her mom.

Betrayed by her father, she was also betrayed by her mother. One day her mother accidentally opened the bedroom door, saw what was happening, then turned and quietly closed the door behind her, putting her need for safety and security ahead of her daughter's. Sharon remained loyal even though her rightful protector did nothing to protect her from the years of abuse that followed.

Sharon never learned to set appropriate boundaries because at the time when her parents should have set boundaries for her and made sure she was operating safely within them, they were proving she had no boundaries at all—not even the sanctity of her own body. This is what she learned at home in her family; this is what was familiar. And these were the holograms she unconsciously kept playing out in her life.

Releasing the Lock

Remembering is different from updating. When you remember, you reexperience the old scene from the same perspective. But in an update it is essential that you reexperience the old scene from as many perspectives as you can: from your perspective as a friend, family member, and neighbor; from the perspective of what experts such as teachers, preachers, counselors, and police would do; from your perspective as an adult.

This time you will be the writer, director, and actor. This time you will be revisiting that scene not just from your limited First- or Second-Gear perspective but from a Third-Gear perspective as well. You will be reexperiencing it as the leader of your life, the one who is responsible for your success now, in the future, *and* in your past. What would you do differently now? And what would you want other people to do differently too?

Life presses us to become more of who we are, but will we let ourselves become more? And will we let other people become more, too? Or will we continue imagining them as they were twenty, thirty, or forty years ago; will we continue insisting they will never change? Do we have our camera fixed in one position, only allowing us to experience that scene one way—keeping us stuck?

What did Sharon need her parents and caretakers to do in that scene? Even though the answer to this question may seem obvious to us, it took Sharon weeks before she could *imagine* her parents being responsible for her safety and protection, before she could *imagine* them as people she could trust. Even trying on those thoughts was disorienting and upsetting, because in order to imagine that reality, Sharon had to release the lock she had put on that scene, the always and never decisions she had made in that moment. But Sharon now understood that she would have to allow herself to become disoriented to heal. She knew staying locked in that old orientation would keep her stuck in a never-ending stream of painful repetitions.

Ask yourself, "What did I need? What gear was I in and what kind of leadership did I need in that scene?"

Sharon discovered that she wanted her mother to be a "lioness" standing guard over her and snarling powerfully—"I'll tear you to pieces if you come near my cub"—even if the person her mother was snarling at happened to be Sharon's father. Before that scene took place, Sharon wanted her father to be her "father protector," the man she ran to with her fears and concerns, the shielder of her body and naïveté, the father who kept his promise that he would be there for her—no matter how tired he felt, no matter how tough his day had been, or how upset he was with her mother, his boss, or their finances. She wanted him to be there for her no matter what. That was his most sacred duty of all.

As Sharon began to update, she realized there were other protectors she could have gone to as well. She thought about what her grandmother, teacher, or preacher might have done *if* she had told them. She played out in her mind and body what it would have been like *if* her aunts and uncles had intervened, or *if* she had gone to the policeman at school. She thought about what he would have said and done. She spent hours seeing other alternatives she hadn't seen that day when, instead of blaming them, she decided, "I must have been responsible for what happened."

No, Sharon, you were not responsible. They were responsible for you.

Updating Loyal

There was another perspective Sharon needed before she would be ready to update. Even though her parents didn't protect her, she remained loyal to them. What did Sharon mean by loyal back then? And what does loyal mean to her now?

In First Gear what we mean by loyal is loyal to people and institutions— parents and caretakers, teachers, bosses, presidents, priests, rabbis, and ministers. Loyal to church and to God as we see Him from a First-Gear perspective, as our Caretaker, Protector, Right-Wrong-Good-Bad Rule-Giving God. In First Gear Sharon couldn't imagine being disloyal to her parents and so she couldn't imagine being loyal to herself.

In Second Gear the meaning of loyal shifts; instead of being loyal to people and institutions, we become loyal to results—getting good grades, making teams, getting and keeping jobs, earning money, power, and position—and to a Second-Gear Provider God, a God of Power and Plenty.

In Third Gear what we mean by loyal shifts again. In Third Gear loyal means loyal to self, loyal to dreams, loyal to the whole—to an ever-changing Creator God. In order to update, Sharon would have to let go of her First-Gear perspective.

The Update: Sharon Finally Gave Herself the Protection She Needed

Sharon was ready to go back into that old scene. Finally Sharon was able to see that bedroom door open and hear herself screaming for *help!* Finally she felt her mother react. She saw the eyes of "the lioness" right there in front of her, claws bared and ready to protect her *no matter what.* She heard her mother clearly spell out to her father, and God, what Sharon's boundaries were. *No one! Never! Ever!* Sharon watched her mother call the police and heard her telling Sharon's grandmother and family, teacher, and preacher what had happened. Together they created a support system for Sharon, set up boundaries, and regularly patrolled them, checking and rechecking, selecting and reselecting who was allowed in her life.

Finally in that update, Sharon experienced unequivocally that she deserved to be protected and sheltered. She deserved to be skillfully led. This is the right of every child on our planet. That is the responsibility of every adult on our planet. No matter what—each child needs to be able to trust that he or she will be protected in the First Gear of life.

Updated Thinking Leads to Updated Results

After feeling protected in that old scene, Sharon noticed places where she needed to be protected now. She had been trying to let go of her secretary, Beverly, for months. She had already hired a new one, but personnel insisted that Sharon keep Beverly on until they could find her another job. With Beverly there, Sharon's time was constantly eaten up in correcting her mistakes and holding her hand, even though she had already been there for eighteen months. And now her new secretary was getting pulled into doing the same thing.

Sharon had just received the defining call. A colleague told her that the reason Beverly was still there was because she had refused two jobs that met her needs exactly! Sharon could see that Beverly was doing what her mother had done. She preferred to remain in First Gear instead of making the changes needed. She preferred to sacrifice Sharon's needs to meet her own. But this time Sharon wasn't a helpless child; this time she was taking control.

Minutes later, when Sharon walked into her boss's office, he immediately knew she would quit if she didn't get his support now. So instead of delaying or delegating, he put aside what he was busy doing and stepped up to the plate, assuring Sharon he would take immediate action. And he did, heading out the door of his office with Sharon right behind him, over to the vice president of personnel. "I want you to let go of that secretary *now*. . . . *Today*. Do you hear me? Enough is enough." A week later Beverly was gone, and Sharon's productivity began climbing.

When updated thinking begins to create updated results, you can add these successes to your Success File. You need to tell yourself and others your new success story, reseeing, rehearing, refeeling, and reexperiencing what just happened over and over.

Sharon called to tell me what she had done but immediately rushed ahead to the next issue. Whoa, Sharon. Slow down! Let's take a closer look at what you just told me—at what happened when you knew exactly what you wanted and you were *unwilling* to settle for anything less. At what you experienced as your boss listened and responded and headed over to the vice president of personnel. The exact words he said when he went to bat for you. And exactly how it felt to have a leader protect you and your interests.

You recharged old failures each time you remembered them. Now you know how to recharge your successes so that they begin automatically and unconsciously attracting more of what you want.

Success-File your Updates: What have you been able to reexperience and redecide? What changes have you made as a result? Who were you able to move through an upset with? What friendships and relationships have you been able to renew? What old scenes have you been able to make sense of? Which gear were each of you in? What did these upsets teach you about how *you* want to live and lead others?

In Third Gear We Are Responsible for Setting Our Own Boundaries

In First Gear our parents, teachers, and bosses are responsible for setting our limits for us—how much play or work is enough before we need to eat or rest, before our shift is over, or the office closes and we have to go home to take care of ourselves and our families. Today, in a world of modems, E-mail, and the Internet; cell phones, beepers, and faxes; and ever-accelerating Second-Gear pressures, you must shift into Third Gear and set limits for yourself. In a Second-Gear society it is easy to overwork, to keep piling on more and more, to be more loyal to your results than to yourself, your family, and dreams. Results are what is rewarded, praised, and promoted.

In Third Gear you are the person who needs to protect you. You are the person who needs to decide when enough is enough, when you need to eat and rest, when you need to put attending your child's ball game or spending time with him or her before bedtime ahead of producing results at work. You are the only one who can send the message to your next generation that you have boundaries and you will be there to set boundaries for them.

Is Your Foundation in Place?

Until our First-Gear needs are complete—whether they're completed by our leaders or ourselves—we can't successfully lead others through First Gear, the gear of old fears and uncertainties, the gear of can't, shouldn't, and impossible, the gear when time and skillful supervision is needed. With incompletions in our lives, like a pan of water sloshing, we tend to rush too far to one side or the other, rarely meeting our needs or others'. Instead we try to do for them *what wasn't done for us*, or we do to them *what was done to us*. We play the role of either the victim or the perpetrator, because with those incomplete holograms still in mind, we keep on attracting those situations over and over.

What can you do to make sure your First-Gear needs are met now? As an adult in First Gear, you must check out the safety and effectiveness of every new situation or relationship before proceeding—before making agreements and commitments, before firming up plans and getting under way. What must you look for to assure you are safe? How long should you say no and keep up your guard or have other people supervise? The answer is, until you know you are safe. Until you know the boundaries you set are observed and respected. Until you know you can express your needs and be responded to supportively. Until you know you are being given the time and attention you require. Until you know this person is dreaming of your success. Until you know it is safe for you to be who you are in that relationship or situation.

Leading is living beyond your own skin, beyond your own perspective. It includes the perspectives of your parents or children, friends or spouses, boss or employees. Which gears are they in, and what is your responsibility to them? Are they dependent on you to protect them and set boundaries for them, to listen and support them, to dream their success with them, to make time to be with them, to support their dreams over yours? And what is their responsibility to you? What gear are you in when you interact with each of them?

The Power of Struggle: The Butterfly That Couldn't Fly

Imagine that you are seated near the front of a theater. The curtains have just opened, and on stage someone is sitting in a chair waiting for a butterfly to emerge from its cocoon. Whether we cast our observer in the role of parent, teacher, or dreamer, male or female, young or old, is not important. The point is, as she watches the butterfly struggling to break free of its protective cocoon—tugging, squirming, shoving, tearing its way out bit by bit—she grows worried. The butterfly seems to be engaging in so much unnecessary effort that our caring observer decides to get up, walk over to a small cupboard, and get a tiny pair of scissors out of the drawer. Returning to her chair, she carefully snips open the cocoon to allow the butterfly to emerge more easily. Days pass. But each day as she watches, the butterfly is still crawling around its box, wings still furled tightly against its body. Even as it nears the end of its life its wings have not opened.

Finally, head in hands, our observer confronts an essential truth: All that effort and struggle, all that working to break free of its incubative confinement was creating the very pumping action needed to press fluids into those wings, to force them to unfold and fill up. But without allowing the butterfly to exert all that effort, instead of flying where it wants the butterfly will be forced to spend the rest of its life on the ground.

So, too, if all your needs had been perfectly met in First Gear, you would still be safely and securely living within the territory that gear defines. If all your needs had been perfectly met in Second Gear, you would still be competing in that territory—no matter how hard the struggle or how great the cost. But the nature of the human process is such that *no one* can ever meet your needs perfectly, no matter how caring, skillful, and compassionate he or she is, and it is up to each one of us to realize that our greatest disappointments press us to fly.

What Should You Update?
Exploring Others' Stories to Find Yours

What scenes in your life are still incomplete? When were your needs unmet? Exactly what did you need from your leaders in that moment?

From time to time an old scene may come to mind and stir up old feelings, but what usually alerts us is *resistance*—I can't, you can't, I don't want to, you don't want to, I don't have time, you don't have time. Whether we blame ourselves or others, we know that something is holding us back.

How can you locate your incompletions? How can you follow the ripples back to their source? One of the best ways is to listen to other people's stories and see what old feelings they dredge up. Notice what your Razz (the part of the brain that compares new and old holograms) brings to mind as you read them.

Like raindrops, memories lay down interference patterns across your brain, but occasionally a rock is thrown into your pond, sending out waves that overwhelm the usual pattern of ripples. We have all had rocks hurled into our lives when inexplicable life events occurred, when leaders let us down. Perhaps the stories I am telling you will remind you of experiences you may want to update.

A Chat with My Mother: Asking the Question I Could Never Ask as a Child

Why did my mother become an alcoholic? This question had bothered me for years. I could guess at the answer, but I wanted to hear it from my mother's perspective. So one day I asked her to sit down at the kitchen table with me. "Mom, why did you drink?" And she told me a story I had never heard before:

"My brother was my best friend, the person I most loved in the world. One day when I went to look for him, I found him lying in a pool of blood on the floor in his room. The shot that killed him wounded my safety and enthusiasm. It prevented me from finishing college and made me afraid to look clearly at life. I began drinking to block the pain. Susan, that shot wounded you as well. I was your mother and I wasn't able to be strong and encouraging for you. I wasn't able to be protective and clearheaded for you. Your question shocked me when you first asked it, but now I feel relieved, relieved that I can finally tell you the truth. It wasn't because I didn't love you. I did. It wasn't because I didn't want to be there for you. I did. It was because I didn't know how. I'm sorry."

And I finally understood.

A Conversation with My Father: The One We Would Have Had If He'd Been Able

Not all conversations can take place in reality. Updating gives you the opportunity to complete conversations in the virtual world. It allows you to complete for yourself what someone else wasn't willing or able to complete for you. It allows you to recover the energy you need to move ahead to your dreams.

Even though my dad happily took me on train rides and around the corner to the fire station when I was a child, when I became a teenager and he no longer agreed with my dreams, he began stridently disagreeing with and preventing my choices. So, instead of reaching out to my dad for support and expertise, I began hiding my dreams from him.

I didn't understand where my father was coming from then. I didn't understand until a generation later when I had teenagers and their choices started scaring me, too. I could see them walking into walls and heading over cliffs I had long since learned to avoid.

It is only now—all these years later and many years after his death—that I can finally *imagine* what I wished my dad had been able to say to me that last day at the hospital when, with nothing said, he was wheeled off to surgery.

Here are the words I had my father speak in the update: "Susan, like the observer on that stage, I couldn't stand to see you writhing and struggling. I couldn't watch as little by little you worked your way out of the cocoon your mother and I had built for you, out of the rules and limits we had taught you. I worried about you more and more as you stepped boldly into unknown territory. But I didn't understand that, like that butterfly, you were transforming into a different you and I needed to be transforming into a different me, a parent who no longer chose for you but who supported you in following through with your own choices. I am proud you had the strength and courage to continue pressing energy into your wings. I am only sad I couldn't have enjoyed the process with you."

And I replied, "I know you would have told me that if you had been able to. I love you, Dad."

A Last Look Back . . .

What limits have been more important to you than living your dreams? What have you needed to be right about more than finding solutions? What confinements and protections have mattered more to you than getting there? Sounds silly, doesn't it, but it's true. And what limits do people close to you have that are more important than supporting your dreams? What rights and wrongs, goods and bads, have-tos and musts, always and nevers? What limiting values do they have that you have learned to live within, too? What fears, jealousies, and insecurities has the threat of your stepping beyond these limits created in them and in you? When have you failed because leaders didn't support you or tried to prevent you? When did you put out tremendous effort but not succeed, or, believing you would fail, fail to try at all?

With Skill 6 in place and the major incompletions of your life updated, huge chunks of long-tied-up energy will be released. You will feel more enthusiastic and eager, more energetic and positive. Instead of dreading and avoiding, you will begin dreaming and intuiting. Chance events will begin happening; hunches will start jolting and jabbing you. Why? Because your Razz is now working on a new set of incompletions—not past ones but future ones. It is working on your dreams. It is beginning to call your attention to opportunities all around you. With Skill 6 in place you can begin to allow serendipity and chance to guide you instead of blocking these wondrous workings of your mind. Now, instead of method-bound, you become outcome-oriented—oriented toward living your dreams.

Skill 7 is committing to outcome. With more energy available and fewer unconscious ties to the past, you are ready to begin listening to hunches and intuitions. Ready to step out on that limb and over to your dream.

Skill 7

Committing to
Outcome

AND ALLOWING

CHANCE AND

SERENDIPITY TO

GUIDE YOU

was on my way to New York for an interview with Lou Dobbs on
CNNfn's *Business Unusual.* For several weeks the producer and
I had been coordinating a training in a Wall Street financial
institution so that they could tape me at work. Finally she had the
details worked out and a video crew lined up for Monday.

But Sunday afternoon, just as I closed my suitcase and checked
outside for my cab, she phoned me with urgency in her voice:
"Susan, your Monday-morning video shoot is off! Your client just
called. The director you were planning to work with died in the
night. His team won't be available either. They'll be at his funeral
on Monday. Do you still want to come? Or would you like to postpone your interview until a better time?"

"No, I'm coming," I said. "I'm on the way to the airport now."
And I immediately began calling other clients in New York, but no

one was available to do a Monday-morning video shoot. Just then my cab pulled in my driveway and I headed for the airport knowing that—somehow or other—I would have a group for tomorrow's shoot.

Boarding the plane, I excused myself as I climbed over the man seated on the aisle and quipped with the man slumped next to the window. They were business partners returning from their annual two-week get-away-from-it-all in the Everglades—no phones, no computers, no work—just relaxing, reconnecting, and redreaming. Then why were they sitting apart? And, just as I had that thought, the man to my left warned me that his partner by the window snored like a sawmill. And he hoped I was up to it.

A few minutes into the flight, we began swapping professional details and I learned they owned a major New York PR firm. I explained my dilemma and my absolute intention, and by the time we landed in New York I had *their* team lined up to do the shoot with me on Monday. Whew! But when I arrived in the CNN studio the next day, Lou Dobbs was out sick so Valerie Morris interviewed me instead. She was a warm and generous interviewer, but afterward I noticed I was a little disappointed. I had been looking forward to meeting Lou Dobbs, but I put it out of my mind. Several weeks later I got a call from Lou's office inviting me to have dinner with Lou and his executive team so that I could tell them about *The Technology of Success* in more detail.

I had just flown in from England. Jet-lagged and time-lagged, I told them, with a laugh, that if they wanted to hear anything, we would have to order dinner right away! Over a delicious Chinese meal at Ma's, I revealed one Success Skill after another as Lou beamed and nodded agreement. Then, as we were gathering our belongings to leave, Lou invited me to come back on the show so he could interview me himself.

After the show, Lou and his staff invited me to teach all levels of his staff *The Technology of Success.* Working with Lou's team over the next year was yet another high-profile validation of the ten skills I had discovered amid years of twists and turns in the road.

With Your Past Complete, Your Razz Focuses on Completing Dreams

C an you hold your outcome—your mission, commitment, goal, task, or dream—all the way to completion? Can you see the forest for the trees? Or will obstacles and interferences become reasons to give up? Will discomfort and disagreement dissuade you or change your mind? Which outcome will you wind up with? The outcome you created or an outcome from First or Second Gear? Or an outcome someone else had in mind for you that you might not want anymore?

In Skill 7, you are building momentum and finding methods. This is when magic slips in, when chance, hunch, and serendipity are available, when realizations wake you in the night or a stranger says something that—Boom!—brings you to solution. Your Razz doesn't care *how*, only *what*.

This is the juicy part of success, the part that makes it exciting and enlivening. Having updated your past and experiencing less resistance, you head toward your outcome at accelerating speed. You're enthused. You're charged. You're tapping into the Universal Hologram—knowing things you don't ordinarily know, doing things you don't ordinarily do. You're in the flow.

The power of your holographic dream/outcome is profound if you trust it. It will bring opportunities that far exceed the limits of your logical mind. As long as you hold on to your outcome, your Razz works in wondrous ways that your First- and Second-Gear mind-sets might refuse to engage in and would even attempt to invalidate by ignoring hunches and overriding insights.

But to continue moving toward your outcome, you will need to be flexible about methods. In First and Second Gears you were focused on *how*—*how* to please leaders and give them what they want and *how* to produce results that would earn you good grades, promotions, and raises. You relied on methods you had learned in the past. But to succeed in Third Gear you will have to move beyond these constraints. *In Skill 7 you are focused on the outcome you want. This is the space in which inventions occur and new ideas are spawned.*

There's an electrical sizzle you will learn to recognize when you're in your Third-Gear creative space—a charge, an inner knowing or certainty that highly successful people describe over and over: "I didn't know how, I just knew that I would." With an outcome clearly in mind, instincts, intuitions, and chance events start aligning with your outcome. No, it's not strange or other-worldly; it's simply how your brain works—calling attention to opportunities your logical mind missed.

Cooperating with Obstacles on the Way to Discovery: Trusting the Process

Having interviewed inventors and innovators about how they came up with their discoveries, I found that their answers were often the same: The chemical spilled; the formula overheated; the wrong ingredients were mixed and—Bam!—they *invented* it (from the Latin *inventus* "to come upon"). With a clearly defined outcome in mind, they came upon opportunities, out of the blue.

In 1929 a comet changed course close to Jupiter and was drawn into its gravitational field, fracturing into pieces. One night in 1993 on Palomar Mountain in southern California, David Levy and Gene and Carolyn Shoemaker spent hours getting ready to photograph the comet, only to discover that someone had opened the film box and exposed the film by mistake. It was overcast and seeing the comet was unlikely, but they decided, "What the heck, let's go for it anyway." And they fished out film exposed along the edges but still usable in the middle, proclaiming, "We have nothing to waste but our time."

When Carolyn inspected the film later, there in the middle of their first shot was the comet. This almost-missed photograph heralded a major astronomical event. All over Earth, from July 16 through July 22, 1994, photographers with telescopes watched the twenty-one-part Shoemaker-Levy 9 comet bombard the surface of Jupiter—the first collision of two solar system bodies ever observed. And the news media covered it and showed it to us.

There were even more coincidences connected with this event. Astoundingly, the Galileo probe was in exactly the right place at exactly the right time to record these bulletlike collisions, not because of careful planning and scientific precision but because its launch had been delayed for months: The antennae had been stored too long and failed to open, and as a result Galileo had to be reprogrammed midflight. Where was the comet when Galileo was finally ready? Straight ahead. Galileo was perfectly positioned to record the Shoemaker-Levy comet crashing into Jupiter, leaving a bruise the size of Earth on its surface and sending up a six-mile-high plume. Could all that have happened logically? Obviously not, but with everyone in Third Gear, focused on outcome, the process unfolded magically.

With His Outcome in Mind, He Triumphed over Fear

Dylan, almost seven, had already had eleven laser surgeries on his face. He was born with a birthmark that if left untreated would have become a dark purple raised blemish covering his face like a man's beard. One month after birth, he had his first surgery, not by choice because his parents knew the torment their son would endure if his face remained disfigured.

Every surgery was like preliving his untreated future; an hour after the laser treatment the whole beardlike area would be purple and swollen. It was excruciatingly painful for Dylan's parents to hold down their one-month-old son during that first procedure and, for weeks later, every time his mom took baby Dylan to a mall or out for a walk, people stared not just at him but at her, wondering, Did she beat him or let him fall? But whatever they were thinking didn't come close to the truth.

By the time Dylan was seven, the birthmark was almost gone except for a barely noticeable patch on his left cheek. This time Dylan himself decided to choose surgery. By now he understood what the long-term picture would be if that now easily overlooked patch went untreated. And he also knew exactly how frightening and painful those procedures had been. But like a brave little soldier Dylan stepped up and proclaimed, "I want my face to be perfect. I want another laser surgery."

Months later, as the day of the procedure approached, Dylan was nervous. The night before he was shaking and anxious. Although he hadn't changed his mind about the surgery, he was unable to keep the details of the procedure at a distance. All those memories of bruises, people staring, swelling, itching, and burning came rushing back to him. All those memories of being restrained as the laser struck the tender skin on his face haunted him.

But in the process Dylan had learned a skill highly successful people use consistently. He was more committed to his outcome than dissuaded by momentary fear and discomfort. What he felt in the moment wasn't as important as what he wanted to experience in the future. At age seven Dylan had discovered a skill that would assist him whether he was sitting down to do homework, preparing to take a fall on the soccer field, or completing all the hard work needed to succeed at anything else he wanted. He was a powerful dreamer, communicator, and user of experts; he was skilled at updating old pain—and he could count on himself to stay on course to his outcomes.

All three gears are necessary for success. Dylan's parents handled his First-Gear needs, allowing Dylan to remain in Third. His doctor-father built Dylan's confidence and went to Dylan's school to explain the procedure to his classmates and teachers. His mother reminded him about how successful earlier procedures had been, showing him photos of his ever-shrinking birthmark and helping him visualize it shrinking again—possibly even disappearing.

The next morning in the operating room his outcome triumphed over his fear and Dylan held his arm still as the needle was inserted that would make him fall asleep. Even though he woke from the anesthesia fighting and screaming, even though two weeks later players from a visiting team called Dylan "a grape head" on the soccer field, he sailed through that crucial healing period knowing "I wanted to do it and I did, and I can do it again if I have to."

Commit to Your Outcome and Your Method Will Appear

Highly successful people put outcome ahead of method. If they can't do it one way, they do it another. Whether scientists in pursuit of a comet, customer service professionals solving customers' problems, or parents leading their children to success, they have faith in their ability to achieve their desired outcome—and they don't need to know *how* in advance. If you don't know how, you can ask, and even if no one knows, your Razz will help you find a way: Two men will sit down next to you on the plane and you'll put two and two together and ask them to be in your video shoot, or spoiled film in a box may still be usable in the middle. Or you stumble upon a new product or a new way to view science.

Success-Filing your outcomes: How did you create your most precious outcomes? Was it by a method-driven, logical, step-by-step process, one you were taught to use in First and Second Gears? Highly successful people worldwide consistently tell me it wasn't that way for them. They chuckle about chance meetings and unbelievable coincidences. Let's look at your life.

How did you meet the people you hold dear to your heart? In my life I found them on the phone, bumped into them in a hall or an elevator, admired a ring, or overheard a conversation and joined in.

One was assigned to share my office; another sat down next to me in the dark at a movie. They arrived when I had "relationship" clearly in mind but was focused on something else altogether. They came in from the side, not logically or predictably but magically—in amazing and delightful ways.

How did you meet your best friends? Was the process logical and predictable, or did chance and serendipity provide the method there as well? I found one of my dearest friends when I laid a manuscript on a bench in a locker room and a stranger handed me a phone number in case I needed an editor. Another best friend worked out as energetically as I did in an aerobics class and we giggled about that afterward. Another fell in love with a best friend and moved into my home temporarily. And I met a producer of *The Today Show* when I was up to my neck in warm water.

How did you find your jobs or your career path? Was that process logical or was it unpredictable and surprising? How about your homes and the places you've lived in? Our greatest power as human beings is preexperiencing what we want by letting go of knowing how and allowing ourselves to be guided until we're there. Why do we believe in logic when we get what we want by magic? Perhaps it's an old habit, one we learned in First and Second Gears.

Here are a few questions you need to ask yourself in Third Gear: Am I willing to embrace magic as part of my life? Am I willing to dream passionately and not know how in advance? Can I say, "No, I don't have a clue. But I know I'll be guided, nudged, blocked, and redirected all the way there, if I'm willing." This is the space of creativity and leadership. This is the space of Skill 7.

All the Rest Turned Back

After eight hours of work, I realized something was drastically wrong with my computer. When I reread the final version of my chapter, none of the changes I had spent all day making and meticulously saving were there. Instead my computer had saved each of those changes in a separate file. There were bits and pieces of my day's work all over the place. I was frantic.

After seven tech-support calls, after explaining my problem over and over, each time being told who to call next, after another day's worth of time on hold, I finally found someone who was willing to journey all the way to solution with me. "I may not know how to solve your problem myself," Albert said, "but we work as a team. We will solve it together."

That was not just some line Albert had memorized in a training session; it was the exact course he pursued. Step by step, question by question, suggestion by suggestion, he headed toward solution, leading me with him. When he took control of my computer via the Internet, he found fifteen thousand temporary files clogging my computer's memory. He'd never seen this problem before, and no one who worked with him had either. So he E-mailed its specifics to engineers across the country and spoke with instructors and managers until bit by bit he pieced together a solution and I was up and running again.

Technicians ahead of him turned back when the pages of their manuals didn't immediately spell out a solution. They talked about "team" but didn't use team members' expertise. They said they'd solve my problem but didn't stay committed—just as most people fail to stay committed all the way to their dreams.

Failure frequently occurs in the last quarter inch of a solution where quantity and quality compete neck and neck, and quantity wins out. From a First- and Second-Gear point of view, this problem was impossible—this problem was new. It required shifting into Third-Gear creativity and cooperation.

In First Gear our most urgent outcome is feeling safe and taken care of. In Second Gear our most compelling outcome is productivity and efficiency. Only in Third Gear does completing what we have in mind become the highest outcome.

Time is money in Second Gear and, to succeed, customer service reps must move on to a problem they can solve more quickly, one that has a solution already. They want to get customers with unique problems off the phone. Why? Because the clock is ticking, and they have fifty-five seconds to handle your call. That's the way their supervisors evaluate their performance; more-better-faster is how they earn raises. So, as customers, we are forced to settle for their productivity instead of the solution we want.

The cost of leaving problems unsolved continues to multiply, tying up even more tech-support hours down the road, wasting more customer time and confidence, and reducing future sales. Imagine if customer service reps understood and were empowered to meet our needs in all three gears. That was the experience I had with Albert, one I hope to enjoy more and more.

The Child Within Always Chooses First-Gear Solutions

Not long ago, I was pulling out of the gas station that I regularly use. The light was green as I entered the intersection but turned yellow immediately. Then the cars ahead of me stopped, blocking me in the intersection as the light turned red, and cars on either side came at me like raging bulls. In that moment my only safe choice was to turn left, even though I had proceeded straight through that no-left-turn intersection for years.

The moment I turned, a police siren screamed at me from behind and forced me over, blocking the driveway to a 7-Eleven. An enraged policeman demanded my license as though I had just killed several people. "That really scared me," I responded. "Give me a second." He never asked why I was scared and walked off in a huff to write up not one ticket but two: no left turn and turning on red. When he finally came back, I tried to tell him what had happened, but he barked, "You can contest those tickets in court," then strode away.

So when the citations arrived, I asked for a court date and

began scripting and rehearsing what I would say to the judge. I wanted both tickets to be dismissed. The traffic flow had failed me. I'd been forced to turn left. I hoped the judge would honor the intent of the law and not a method that failed to work in that situation. A few weeks later, while attending a town council meeting, I was told the Department of Transportation was rerouting traffic because so many cars were getting trapped in that intersection. I felt more certain than ever that both tickets would be dismissed.

On the appointed day, I walked into court committed to my outcome, but the court I walked into wasn't the one I expected. This was a pretrial hearing: "If you plead no contest and don't ask for a trial, we'll make you a deal you simply can't refuse." When I was called and I told the hearing officer "my truth," she acknowledged that the intersection was a problem, reduced the fine to the bare minimum, and took away the points on my license. Her deal felt good in that moment, and I heard myself say, "Okay. That's fine. I just wanted to be heard."

But when I paid the fine and read the receipt, it said right there in black and white that I was *guilty*. I was sick to my stomach. I had sold out on my outcome—I had failed to get those tickets dismissed. Why? Was it because I was scared, and I wanted it over? Was it because it would be my word against that overpowering policeman's in court? Was it because I was afraid the result would be something far worse? Then, as though the universe intended to drive home the point of my retreat even more forcefully, while I was standing in the hall looking at the word *guilty*, the bailiff from the hearing came over to me and said, "I wouldn't have settled my case if I were you. You would have had both tickets dismissed if you had asked for a trial."

I couldn't sleep for a couple of nights, smacked in the face by how powerful survival, safety, and judgment are. First Gear fears frequently drown out our dreams. Whether we are sitting in the dentist chair or confronting a policeman or a judge, the child inside us goes for First-Gear safety and correctness instead of our adult outcome.

Third Gear Is Unreasonable:
You Never Know How You'll Get There

Remember Lillian and her little puppy named Fuzzy? Here's an update. In search of a new job in a new industry, Lillian decided, given her unique skills, preferences, and talents, she would explore working as a medical recruiter. After talking to all of the recruiters she knew and getting their slant on exactly what the industry was like, she settled on what seemed like her ideal job: recruiting nurses. Lillian loved working with women, and she thought guiding nurses to the jobs they wanted would be fulfilling. She settled on one company everyone recommended as the best in the industry. But when she interviewed for the position, her hologram was shattered and she became confused. In reality the job had a very small advance on commissions, and, even though by next year she would be making enough money, it would take months for her to make even *close* to what she was spending.

So Lillian veered off course a bit, accepting a position recruiting doctors instead: radiologists and anesthesiologists, who turned out to be extremely busy and hard to get on the phone. She was told to tell the doctors' secretaries that they were expecting her call. It was painful for Lillian to do this, because when the doctors finally did come to the phone, they were annoyed and even angry. That was the nature of the cold calls she made every day. And even when she found the precise positions they wanted, they weren't grateful to Lillian or even nice. She didn't even get a thank-you. It was a million miles away from the fulfilling, relationship-building conversations she'd had in mind and the feeling of knowing that her clients were happy she'd helped them.

Besides, Lillian was used to setting her own schedule, managing her own goals, and meeting them consistently. But her insecure boss was telling her exactly what to do and when to do it—even though she was producing results and bringing in profitable contracts. In every meeting she was *dinged* for not following procedures exactly. Then came September 11, and while everyone else's results fell to nothing, Lillian's held up. But instead of acknowledging her performance, her boss *dinged* her again. Lillian gave up. No, she didn't quit the job (she couldn't afford to), but she did quit trying. For months she anxiously waited for her boss to fire her. But her results were holding up so, even though other people were fired, she was kept on. Finally she went in to tell her boss she wasn't happy, thinking for sure that would trigger her firing. But she offered to transfer her to another department with the kind of manager she wanted, and temporarily relieved, Lillian said yes.

Now Lillian she was recruiting cardiologists. They were even harder to get on the phone and even more outraged when she tried to talk to them. After a reasonable number of months, she decided to resign (delete the job). She cleaned out her desk and took her birthday off. When she came in the next day, her manager asked to see her. Of course, Lillian was sure she was being fired, but there was yet another twist in the road. When she told her new manager the whole story—how she had originally wanted to recruit nurses and ended up recruiting doctors, how she wanted to build relationships but ended up working with people who didn't even want to pay the company—she asked Lillian if she wanted to transfer to recruiting nurses instead. Her manager would make the contacts for Lillian and set everything in place. And since Lillian would be staying with the company, the months she had been there would count and her health insurance would continue uninterrupted.

Lillian's head was spinning. There she was all packed up to leave and she was being offered the very job she had wanted in the beginning but couldn't afford to take. On the same day, she had received a call from the owner of a company in her old industry who wanted to hire her and was willing to pay her whatever she wanted. She was tempted again. But this time she solidly grabbed ahold of her dream, recruiting nurses, and trusted the miraculous way she had been guided there. After a day of rethinking and reconstructing her holograms, she said yes. By a very unexpected route, she had finally gotten the outcome she wanted and she seized the opportunity.

But there's another twist in the story. Lillian called me to discuss her decision on the very day I was making final changes to this manuscript. I had decided to eliminate a story that no longer seemed to fit. I had been thinking about what to replace it with for days, but nothing had hit me. During our conversation I began to feel something shout inside me, *Wait just a minute, Susan. This might be the story.* And I continued listening, knowing an unexpected opportunity had come my way again . . . and my Razz had let me know: *ZZZZZZZZ . . . Pay attention. This is what you need.*

No Matter What, No Excuses, No Exceptions

While I was learning to become a speaker, I attended a training program in New York City that required us to become outcome oriented just to stay in it. Once a month participants flew in from all over the country, and here was the rule: If you arrived late or unprepared, you were out—no matter what happened to your plane or cab or car or elevator or how busy you were with urgent matters. *There were no excuses. You had to deliver or else—the bottom line of a professional.* Session by session we learned to anticipate obstacles and clear away as many as we could in advance. The process of getting there was electrifying as the minutes ticked away between where we were and where we needed to be, as possibilities slipped away because of canceled flights or bad weather.

In the beginning, instead of focusing on handling external obstacles, we wasted energy switching back and forth between dreams and dreads, between what we wanted and what we feared. Little by little we learned to hold on to our holograms. During the years since, I have been most grateful for that training—especially when I was boarding that flight to CNN without having anyone lined up to interview. With the memories from that training program in my mind as a reference point, I venture into the unknown knowing that I can bend time and circumstances to complete my outcome, no matter what.

Parenting is a very similar "training." To succeed at parenting we must commit to guiding our children, no matter how tired we are, how hard a day we had at work, how horrible our cold is, or how pressed we're feeling about money or career. As mothers, we complete an additional nine-month "sensitivity training" up front. We share our bodies and emotions with our child. We surrender our familiar emotions and shapes. We walk past mirrors and see ourselves expanding. We learn to move and bend in unusual ways. And, in those final few weeks and hours, we stretch beyond what *anyone* would consider reasonable. Then, with our miracle finally there in our arms, we are moved to tears and awe. Look at the life we have created together; look at the life we are responsible for leading. No matter what it took, it was worth it.

Whether we are parenting or climbing mountains, the same absolute commitment is essential. As they scaled the Himalayas, a team of climbers made their way across mile-deep crevasses in the ice. Laying an aluminum ladder over each chasm, they inched their way across in their heavy ice boots. Each step was treacherous. Each step had to be impeccably made. And what else was required to be able to cross that short but perilous span? No matter what, they had to focus on the other side. If, for one second, they thought about falling, they would lose their balance and fall. Dreamers, like tightrope walkers, make it across that perilous space by experiencing being there already.

In First Gear, whenever we were frightened and unsure, we asked parents and teachers who knew what we ought to do—or who acted as if they did. In Second Gear, whenever we were frightened and unsure, we looked to our bosses and their evaluations to tell us what to do next. We were following a carefully prescribed course they had laid out for us. Take this step and that and that . . .

and you will receive your degree, promotion, raise, or bonus. But in Third Gear there is no one to ask but you. What do you want? Yes, what do *you* want? That is the other side of the crevasse.

Outcome over method sounds Machiavellian, but it isn't. In Second Gear our outcome is winning, but in Third Gear our approach is cooperative. In the interest of serving customers, we share information and resources; we support and encourage them. We even take a call at 3:00 A.M. to assist a teammate. It is no longer only about our numbers and evaluations, our comfort and efficiency. It's about transcending our own needs to meet the needs of others. As parents we know this space well; it would be far easier to do it ourselves than to assist our kids in learning how, but in Third Gear we are committed to passing on our skills.

Success-Filing outcomes over methods: When have you put outcome over method and gotten results in a most unusual way? When did you listen to your inner guidance? When did you walk a certain way because you had a hunch? When did you take an unorthodox step something inside you just kept urging you to take? And it worked? When did you *not* have an ingredient and make an even better dish? When did "need become the Mother of Invention"? When did you get somewhere on time even though it seemed impossible? When did someone you had been trying to call walk up to you in the hall? Or call you? When did you shake and quake but keep following your instincts anyway?

Creativity Creates Discomfort: Old Pants, Coats, and Shirts

My daughter's living room wall was so large that an ordinary-sized framed picture looked like a postage stamp. So she asked me to help her create a fifteen-by-six-foot wall hanging. In search of the fabrics we would need, I headed for a nearby thrift store and selected three huge bags of velvets, corduroys, and tapestries that came in the form of old pants, coats, and shirts instead of by the yard. Margaret and I giggled as we cut off sleeves and legs and opened them into flat pieces again. Then we stitched together several huge curtains and started cutting abstract fabric shapes and placing them in what we thought were "right" positions. I remember the expression I saw on Margaret's face. "But, Mom, this isn't what I thought it would look like." Instead of the luxurious textural wall hanging Margaret had in her mind, what she saw on the floor in front of her were a couple of old curtains with cutup shirts and pants pinned on top of them. What we were doing was disturbing Margaret's radiologist mind, which was used to set procedures and predictable results.

We were just beginning the creative process, a million miles and methods away from the rich, textured hanging overlaid in luscious suedes and metal pieces we had sketched. As we continued overlaying pieces, I had her step back to look at what we were creating in the context of the whole room. I pointed out what these shapes, colors, and textures were doing. We observed how the hanging was reflecting the colors in her rug and the kilim pillows on her sofa. And finally I saw the light go on in her head: "Aha, I can see it!"

Six hours later we stopped for the day, but what Margaret had learned during those life-changing hours was one of the most important steps in creativity: You have to be able to hold "your rich, textural wall hanging in your mind while you're cutting up old shirts and trousers." You have to be able to hold your outcome in mind as you wend your way through the process of getting there.

One of the reasons people aren't more creative is that they can't stand the tension creativity creates. So they head for the store to buy something that doesn't match their creative desires but feels safer and easier.

Addicted to One and
Only One Method

At age fourteen, when Monica's father invited her to share her first cigarette with him, it felt like a rite of passage. But it wasn't. Instead it was an invitation to travel the same road on which he and her mother would lose their lives, and it would take Monica more than thirty years to walk away from the addiction. For Monica, a cigarette gradually became "someone" she could wake up with in the morning, a way to feel glamorous like the women in the ads, a way to take a break or finish off a meal. When her father died of lung cancer, she was shaken but not enough to question her approach to meeting all those needs. Even after her mother's funeral, she continued to smoke though she forbade her nieces to ever start. Then, on his way to school one day, her seven-year-old nephew called and begged her to stop. "I love you," he sobbed. "I've lost Grandma and Grandpa, and I want you to live." And she finally heard him.

What is an addiction? An addiction is getting fixated on a particular method, whether it is drinking to have fun, taking drugs to relax, being in a particular relationship, or going shopping. Addiction is having one and only one method and fixating on it obsessively. A wise teacher once told me that I needed to think of at least three ways to produce an outcome before taking action; otherwise, I would be robotic and method bound.

The way out of addiction is to become outcome oriented again, the way you were as a child. What other methods, ways, or approaches could give you what you want—plus health and balance?

Acupuncture: A Method I Would
Normally Avoid Like the Plague

Leaving the hospital after a grueling overnight shift, a doctor ran a red light and slammed into my car. My face struck the steering wheel, and I was left bleeding and dazed, the horn blaring.

When the pain and bruising had diminished, I discovered that my left cheek was lifeless: after nine months of tests and failed treatments, it was beginning to look like that numbness would be permanent. As I stared in the mirror and tapped on my cheek, my face felt like wood and I couldn't pull the left corner of my mouth up into a smile. For a happy, smiling person like me that was not okay, and as a professional speaker, it wasn't okay either. I was very clear: I wanted my face to come back to normal—no matter what.

Then an attorney friend told me acupuncture might solve my problem. And I had to face that "no matter what" head-on. Western medicine hadn't worked for me, but acupuncture? "No way, I can't do acupuncture; I hate needles. No, I don't believe in it, and I don't think it's covered by my insurance. No, no, no." But if there was even the tiniest possibility that a method called acupuncture might return my face to normal, I had to try it.

Pressing past fears and logical excuses, I made an appointment with an acupuncturist my friend said was one of the best in the country. When I was called into her treatment room, she took an extensive history and explained to me exactly what she would do and how it would feel. She told me to close my eyes and she quickly and painlessly inserted two needles in my face near the top of my left cheekbone.

Suddenly energy flowed through my face, and within five minutes I had normal sensation again. It was like a circuit breaker had been reset. A miracle? No, a new method, one that produced the outcome I had wanted with all my heart. This method was initially outside "my box"—in the Potential Zone, that previously unsafe territory I avoided like the plague in First Gear and only verged on in Second Gear. Now I was openly choosing to embrace this territory. Why? Because the Potential Zone is where everything we want to experience and enjoy exists—if we have the self-confidence, commitment, and flexibility to venture there.

Bridging the Gap:
Transforming Your Outcome

On the way to outcomes, we frequently find ourselves blocked, redirected, and confused. Has my dream been destroyed, or will it simply manifest itself in another form?

When Brian O'Leary was a boy, he told his teacher he was going to Mars someday. To her this declaration must have seemed like an unlikely possibility. There wasn't a NASA program yet and so going into space would have been hard to imagine. But the year he entered college, Russia launched *Sputnik* and the space race heated up. Ten years later Brian was an *Apollo* scientist-astronaut scheduled to go to Mars. But the Mars mission was canceled, and after getting that close to his dream, Brian would either crash and burn or allow his Razz to guide him to his outcome in transcendent ways.

Brian saw the Apollo program as "a crowning human achievement, an example of what we can do as a nation when we put our minds to it." At NASA he experienced what it is like to engage in an "impossible" dream. He learned to hold on to an outcome no matter what, to press his mind and body beyond fear and panic to alignment, cooperation, and possibility. And he experienced the commitment and teamwork that are required.

In 1979 Brian's journey into space took an unexpected turn. While participating in a personal growth workshop, Brian had an experience that his scientific education and training couldn't explain. He "remotely viewed" a man he'd never met; he described in tremendous detail where he lived and exactly what he did. Afterward he discovered that what he had "viewed" was astoundingly accurate. He was shocked and excited but profoundly disoriented. Based on everything he knew and was teaching at Princeton, stepping into someone else's consciousness shouldn't have been possible. But he had experienced it, and he couldn't deny it.

Instead of outer space, his remote-viewing experience launched Brian into inner space, a far more unfamiliar and uncomfortable place. As the years passed Brian found other hard-nosed scientific colleagues secretly exploring this territory, too. Dr. Robert Jahn, dean of the School of Engineering and Applied Sciences at Princeton, had been pulled outside his scientific box by a senior honors student's project on psychokinesis, or "mind over matter." She tested whether a subject's thinking could affect a device called a "random event generator." After more than a million trials, they found a clear mind-over-matter effect with a chance probability of 1 in 5,000. UFOs, psychic healing, mystical traditions—are these areas science should avoid, or areas science should explore and include?

What are we committed to? Is it knowing and discovering, or is it insisting existing systems are "true" even when we have evidence to the contrary? Remember the three gears of loyalty: loyal to people, loyal to results, and loyal to the whole. Are we more committed to our institutional reputations and our own positions and funding than to the outcomes we have in mind as a society? Are our current methods of manufacturing and competing and winning more important than meeting people's needs and wants?

The word science comes from the Latin *scientia*, "to know." But what are we willing to know? In *The Second Coming of Science*, Brian O'Leary writes, "In confronting 'unexplainable' phenomena, what I learned was that we—scientists and lay people alike—had isolated ourselves in an invisible box of our own making.... As a result we had become prisoners of our own limiting beliefs."*

Other scientists are stepping out of the box, too. Physicist Fred Wolf says that the problem with our scientific way of thinking is

---

* Brian O'Leary, *The Second Coming of Science* (Berkeley, Calif.: North Atlantic Books, 1993) p. 3.

"explanation means a cause-and-effect relationship. If we can't fit something into a cause-and-effect relationship, we surmise that we haven't explained it. This is the notion I'm challenging. Maybe we need a new theory; maybe we need something bigger than just quantum mechanics. I think synchronicity is another ordering parameter of the universe."*

Synchronicity is the ordering parameter of Skill 7—the ordering parameter of Third Gear.

What Outcomes Are You Committed To?

What outcomes are you committed to, not just at the word level but at the action level—the level of making sure they happen by changing schedules, setting up contingency plans, and running the rest of the way?

Let's review the outcomes of each gear: In First Gear our dominant outcome is safety and survival as individuals, families, and nations. In Second Gear our dominant outcome is conquering and acquiring: This is what we want, and we'll fight for it. But have we become so obsessed with winning, money, and power that we have given up our prime values, the principles we say we stand for? Are we sacrificing our children to a Second-Gear God who rewards us for putting work first, arriving home after bedtime and reneging on promises, overlooking subtle cues and intimate conversations? Are we giving our all at work but leaving nothing for realizing dreams?

In Third Gear, what outcomes are you willing to devote time and attention to? What outcomes need to be shielded from personal and corporate gain? What outcomes are you willing to speak out and take heat for, knowing we are all here on this small planet called Earth, a planet we must nurture so she can nurture us?

* Fred Wolf, transcript, IONS Panel, www.noetic.org.

Shielding Your Dream

The only safe place in the long process of implementation is the virtual world, the world of your dreams. But you cannot stay there all the time. You must journey back and forth, stepping into your dream to gain strength and determination and stepping back into reality with the openness and humility of not knowing.

Many leaders head toward their dreams expecting to continue operating in Third Gear, locked in an ivory tower, university think tank, or safely behind closed doors. *Wrong.* If you stay in Third Gear, your dream will remain a dream and fail to become a reality.

In First and Second Gears, your leaders shielded you from life-threatening accidents and errors, but like little Sam, hairbrush in hand and ready to paint, you were frequently talked out of what you wanted, told no, and redirected to what you could or should do instead. Your life may be different now, but those accumulated experiences laid down a powerful unconscious message: "You can't decide for yourself. You need permission. They know but you don't." This heavily reinforced message could become your greatest challenge. It could make you hesitate at the very moment when an opportunity presents itself, at the very instant when you need to take action.

This time, instead of letting others dissuade you, you need to continue inching your way across the treacherous crevasse to the dream world. You need to shield yourself and your Codreamers in the process. You are a leader, leading not just yourself but others. Will you meet their needs for safety and certainty in First Gear and for productivity, assessment, and rewards in Second Gear—or will you get stuck in Third Gear and fail to support your supporters in supporting you?

In Skill 4 you shield your dream. In Skill 8, you shield your Codreamers and Cooperators, those members of your team who are journeying to your dream with you. You know what you have had to go through to get this far in the success process and you must now generously extend an arm and a heart to those who are following you and may be stuck somewhere along the way.

Establishing "The Lock"

Opportunities come in their own time, arriving in moments you least expect them, amid circumstances that seem illogical or impossible. But if you pay attention—and use your dream as a sacred reference point—you will know: *This is it.*

Then you must tether yourself to your dream and take action. Whether it's a new relationship, home, invention, or business, you must confront the same sloshing of emotions one way and then the other: I will. I won't. It is. It isn't. It matches. It doesn't match. You began dreaming in Third Gear but suddenly and inexplicably you find yourself in First Gear again—the First Gear of implementation—right/wrong, good/bad, can/can't, possible/impossible. Old fears and incompletions fill in unclear spaces.

Whenever you present a new idea, you will encounter disagreement, all the reasons why not, why your dream is impossible, why you should abandon this folly and return to life as usual in First and Second Gears.

But you can't. Your old life has been disturbed by this dream. Something you didn't know was missing has been highlighted and must now be included; something that resonates with old fears and disappointments but resounds even more strongly with an alive part you've been incubating for years.

After my daughter Cathy dropped her kids off at school, instead of heading for the highway, she cut through a neighborhood she loved and wandered down its meandering streets, looking and longing. Suddenly a house with a for-sale sign reached out and took her by the heart, but, instead of ignoring that tug, she picked up her cell phone and made an appointment to see it in a half hour.

As she stepped into that house, she stepped into her dream: a seaside cottage with porches and trellises—open, breezy, light—with a living room that extended out endlessly into the backyard. Suddenly Cathy could see her son and daughter playing on an old tire hanging under a broad-armed shade tree. She saw her husband showering in the cathedral-ceiling master bath and herself relaxing with a good book in an Adirondack chair in the lushly planted enclosed brick courtyard. The house was only ten blocks from her kids' school, so the two hours a day she was spending driving north and south to drop off and pick up could be spent in far more productive and enjoyable ways.

But this wasn't a good time to suggest buying a new house to her husband. His business had been through two years of ups and downs and he was struggling to pull out. Good time or not, this house was not something Cathy could let go. With her dream shielded in her heart, she proposed her idea to Alan and he, not wanting to immediately dash her dream but not considering it a reality, agreed to go see it with her on his way home.

It had taken Cathy a little while to get from impossible to possible, and she knew it would take time for Alan to make that transition, too. So with her shield polished and in place, she prepared to protect her dream in the meantime. Objection after objection, negative after negative, he fired bullets at its possibility. But instead of reacting and firing back, she took each bullet gently in her arms and held it, knowing he had one bullet less.

Meanwhile her dream was finding fertile soil in his heart, and he was beginning to try on living there, too. He was moving furniture around mentally, picking a spot for his sound system and TV, measuring the master bedroom for their huge antique bed—all the while discharging his remaining negatives as Cathy continued shielding.

Then the time-and-money discussions began. How much more would that house cost than the one they were living in? Would all their furniture and possessions fit in less space? What would they do for storage without a garage? How much would the move cost? How much less time would it take to get to work or home for dinner? He really liked the location and the neighborhood. Cathy's heart pounded as he came closer and closer to holding her dream with her, closer and closer to its being a shared dream.

But would they be able to sell their old home in time? Fortunately the seller was a Realtor and he agreed to make the contract contingent on selling their house. He would manage the listing so he could expedite the sale. After days of negotiating, offering and counteroffering, they agreed on price and terms and scheduled an open house for the following Sunday, with one added clause—if Cathy found a buyer, she would earn half the commission.

Cathy got on the phone and put out the word to everyone she knew. The next morning she received a call from the brother of a friend who was looking for a house in their neighborhood. He and his wife came to see it that evening and arranged to look at it again two hours before the open house the next day. Cathy watched as they moved furniture around in their minds and decided about renovations and wall colors. Even though they tried to act disinterested, she could feel the vibe—this was their house. The next day her friend confirmed her intuition, and as a steady crowd of prospective buyers paraded through that first open house, they made an offer Cathy and Alan couldn't refuse. The house was sold.

But the need for Cathy to shield her dream didn't stop there. The owner of Cathy's new house was expecting a baby in mid-May. The couple buying her house was expecting a baby a few weeks later, and their shields began to clash. Her buyers were pushing to close May first. Her broker-seller was shoving to close by the end of May, and Cathy—the only more or less neutral party regarding time—was in the middle.

Caught up in shielding his wife and baby, her broker-seller pushed back too hard, almost killing the deal. Shielding everyone's dreams, Cathy navigated her way through days of possibilities proposed, rejected, reproposed, and finally accepted. With only four weeks till their move, she jumped into action, planning, sorting, and donating.

There's a Time Lag in the Universe

Realities require far more time and effort than dreams. Dreams exist immediately in the holographic universe, but the process of building them in time and space requires far more tenacity and persistence. That ephemeral thing called a dream, unless prelived and regularly detailed, will simply shape-shift into another form, leaving you frustrated and incomplete, feeling like a failure.

You are the leader and protector of your dream. As you get closer to its reality, you must shield your dream from threatening forces and thoughts, obstacles and setbacks, and time and money pressures. Leadership isn't just about Third Gear; it's about using all three gears appropriately. And this is the challenge. As dreamers, we created our outcome in Third Gear, energized by it, confident, surrounded by Codreamers, communicating and gathering expertise, with our fears updated for the moment. But then suddenly we find ourselves in First Gear again, childlike and dependent. *This is to be expected.*

This is the First Gear of implementing your dream. You ventured into the Potential Zone in Third Gear, but now you find yourself out there in the void in First Gear, facing your fears and others' fears simultaneously: good/bad, can/can't, possible/impossible. Will you choose comfort instead of your dream? Will you insist on familiar methods or stay open to far more useful timings and methods when they serendipitously present themselves?

As You Shield Others, Your Dream Will Shield You

We want someone there with us as we inch our way along toward our dream. But even the best partners are not always there. Even the most aligned Codreamers have their own blocks and limits, fears and uncertainties. Even in the most crucial moments phone lines go dead, computers go awry, and usual ways of reaching out are unavailable.

Who will shield you as you shield everyone else? Your dream will shield you. *Fortunately a gift comes to the dreamer:* As you pursue your dream you have a different body chemistry—more energy, endurance, focus, and joy, not just about the completion but about the process itself. And everything in your life is infused with that glow.

No matter how far out there in the virtual world you go, you must simultaneously remain grounded in the here and now, shielding your own body and mind, continuing to take productive steps and manage responsibilities. As you inch closer, you feel the tension increasing between the here and now and your dream. Can you keep yourself solidly grounded on both sides of the crevasse until you make it across? Or will you let go of one side or the other and let that bridge fall?

To sustain yourself, you will need to revisit your dream regularly. Or else, finding yourself midair, you will fall under the effects of your usual First- and Second-Gear reality and slip into life as usual.

You Must Shield Yourself as You Journey from Virtual to Real

According to the dictionary, a shield is a broad piece of leather or metal held to protect the body from arrows, spear thrusts, and blows. A shield is also something or someone that serves to defend or protect. Your home shields you from weather and intruders; your car shields you from the forces of acceleration and deceleration; your dreams shield you from uncertainty and confusion—they give you direction and power.

Returning from the virtual world, you will need shields as you reenter the gravity of creating at the physical level: the gravity of other people's ideas and the time and energy creation will actually take. Using Skills 1 through 7, you have overcome your own inertia, but now you will be encouraging more and more people to "take the heat" with you. As a leader, you will need to shield those who travel to your dream with you, to protect them from the resistance new ideas generate. And you must be willing to allow others to shield you as well.

Shielding presses you to understand the gears from the other side, to remember exactly what First Gear was like for you, what your needs were. It encourages you to do unto others what you would have them do unto you—if you were in the same gear. It takes you into the realm of relationship and urges you to communicate which gear you're in so that others can be sensitive to your needs—not the ones you had this morning when you were up and eager, but the ones you have after a frustrating meeting or a series of incompletions.

This shield is different from the ones we use in war. This shield is like a glass globe you would put over a seedling. Its purpose is to create a supportive environment while your dream sends down roots and puts out stems and leaves—until your dream has gained enough strength for you to take that globe off and let it grow on its own, still keeping a watchful eye. Your teammates are just beginning to codream and cooperate, and they will need support as they go through the process step by step. You will need to model these skills. You will need to teach them these skills. And in the meantime, you will need to shield them from taking on too much too soon, from too much disapproval and failure, from too much competition and power.

As we sped along the interstate, seven-year-old Dylan was showing his younger sister Eliza how to use his Gameboy. Part of him genuinely wanted to slow down so that Eliza could learn, but part of him was unable to shift into First Gear, competing with her instead. "Oh, Eliza, that's so easy. You don't know how to do that? Look how fast I can." He was showing her halfheartedly, not wholeheartedly gearing back to where she was, unable to meet her needs because they were not his. Her concerns seemed trivial as he raced ahead to his next level.

Shielding is about supporting and protecting Codreamers and Cooperators as they shift up and down through the gears of a dream. It requires you to understand the Success Gears from the other side, to remember what First Gear was like, how much attention and encouragement you needed. And, yes, to remember how different it felt when you shifted into Second Gear, how much freedom and feedback you wanted. And it presses you to ask them exactly what they need from you.

Discovering New Love:
The Terrifying Potential Zone

After years of dreaming, here it is: a sudden inexplicable feeling, an electric current that cannot be ignored. Though it makes no sense in this context, its power keeps growing. The voice. The pace. The curve of the words. Will I override the signals that have intensified my pulse and senses? Will I sacrifice this fragile offering to the winds and tides? Or will I shield it and nurture it? And will he?

As we continue talking, our questions and answers press us past the point of "normal" almost imperceptibly—and my feelings amplify each incremental change by the thousands. Or am I mistaken?

I am tracing a golden thread, but where is it leading? What emotions must I include to keep moving its way—fear, confusion, doubt, embarrassment, the risk of letting out more feelings than I can pull back inside without leaving a gaping hole? Will I continue inching forward or turn back now? Confronting the polarities— the most exciting, the most terrifying—taking one step forward. Shaken by my boldness and fragility—wanting to turn back to safety and familiar territory. A pan of water sloshing—rushing out boldly and retreating terrified, feeling the response nurturing and encouraging me out there again. It is painful sustaining this excruciating risk but moving ahead anyway. Could I be wrong—is it only going on over here? Or could it be going on over there, too?

Will all this energy that has been stirred up need to be shoved, not so neatly, back into the box of how my life has been? As we continue talking, I begin expressing cloaked doubts and he reassures me. I am even more frightened but magnetized, knowing my heart will not let go now even though I tell myself I should. Could I bear the pain if I am wrong about "impossible"? As we each proceed cautiously, his questions begin to subtly diverge from their expected course. Tiny little hints—or am I making them up?—seem to guide me toward him, a dance so subtle and imperceptible that my pounding heart will burst either way. But the boundaries of uncertain and unspoken are rapidly approaching. In a few minutes we could end this encounter and never meet again. I am bound by circumstances, but he is not. Will he reach out? And in one explosive moment, he does.

Phone numbers are exchanged.

Love and Passion Are Essential in Third Gear

Whether you are hot on the trail of a new relationship, career, home, or scientific breakthrough, the rules of engagement have changed. In First and Second Gears, even love had to operate according to prescribed rules. The person we met had to be a certain age, dress and talk in a certain way, make a certain amount of money, and live according to familiar (remember, the word *familiar* comes from the word *family*) methods, or he or she was out of the question. And it was the same with friends, homes, and dreams; they had to conform or they were eliminated as possibilities. We were so method bound that we abandoned our outcomes, like romance and communication and compatibility.

But in Third Gear your outcome is more important than your method or theirs, and you willingly brave the disapproval of people who continue to shout the old message: But you can't live in that neighborhood. But you can't make statements like that at this university. But you can't go out with someone younger or older. In Third Gear their resistance simply becomes a part of the process, a step along the way. When you hear that siren call, you fly to the virtual world to revisit your dream and strengthen yourself. *This feels right to me. And I am going to pursue it.*

Romance and passion are essential in Third Gear. We must be in love with our dream, passionate about its gestation, and absolutely committed to its birth—or else the world of the *familiar* will overwhelm us. Like Dr. Karl Pribram's, Tiger Woods's, or Oprah's, your dream must burn in your heart.

You Will Need to Shift Your Shielding Voice Up and Down

In Second-Gear competition we are frequently so preoccupied with productivity that we fail to remember that the foundation of success is meeting First-Gear needs first: making sure others feel safe, fed, and protected up front; answering all their questions immediately; breaking ideas and actions into easily succeed-able steps; acknowledging them warmly and consistently; and, above all, protecting them from danger—internal and external.

First Gear: The Voice of the Protector

We shield in three voices; each one has its own pitch, tone, and pace that we must recognize and cherish. The first voice speaks in support of First-Gear success: the protective parent, a friend standing by you in rough times, a nurturing manager making sure that you are eating and resting, and that you feel certain. Whether you are a new lover who talks about HIV testing before sex or a loving partner who asks whether your beloved ate, slept, exercised, or remembered to lock the door, your focus in that moment is safety, security, and health.

When my daughter Cathy was an infant, my husband and I

were driving along a country road one foggy night when we rounded a bend and saw a car stopped ahead in the road with no lights. By the time we had processed the thought, we were crashing into him, and I held on to our infant daughter with every fiber of my being.

The accident happened before there were laws mandating car seats and seat belts, and the only thing shielding our child from being thrown inside or outside our car was my body. Whatever it took, I was committed to keeping her safe—and what it took was several years of excruciating neck pain and restraining Thomas collars. But, like a lioness protecting her cub, I shielded Cathy from serious injury, and that was all that mattered in the moment.

Today we shield our children in more aggressive ways. We install door locks and toilet-seat latches. We have industry standards for clothing, cribs, and toys. We teach our children to dial 911 as soon as they can talk and rehearse what to do if someone comes to the door or touches them inappropriately. We hire professionals to childproof our homes.

But in these busy times, it is easy to forget about shielding ourselves. In this protector voice, we ask questions and anticipate needs. "Are you okay? You seem exhausted. Did you eat breakfast? Do you need a break?" Or an observant supervisor quips, "I've seen you around here too much lately. Take some time off." Or a teammate trips on a retaining wall and gashes his shinbone; his teammates transport him to the hospital, take over his job functions, and follow up the next day to make sure he's on the mend.

Questions like "Did you eat or sleep?" and "What do you need from me?" are questions we need to ask not only our children but also our mates and coworkers. Those questions remind us to attend to First-Gear needs first, because we know we won't be productive and creative when we're scared, exhausted, or ill.

And we must shield our teammates from fears, comforting them when they wake up from scary dreams, experience upsets past and present, and experience change and an uncertain future.

We can go back virtually into old scenes, giving them what they wanted and needed then, filling in holes, updating and releasing energy. And we can move ahead into future success scenes with them as well: "You are going to do a great job today. You are well prepared."

Handling Safety and Comfort First: Taking Someone by the Hand

As you build a professional or personal relationship, your ability to shield your partner creates the foundation for what you will be able to do—how high, deep, and far you can go, how many dreams you can enjoy. Will your ventures together generate confidence and trust or press you to avoid each other in the future?

What had made my tech-support call to Albert so successful? He spoke to me in the protector voice. That was exactly the voice I needed to hear in that moment. I was in First-Gear fears. The file that contained my book was disappearing in front of my eyes and, after a whole day of failed calls and futile suggestions, I was exhausted and still losing data. Albert asked me where I was and where I wanted to be and played back what I had said so I knew that he knew and he could begin using his expertise to assist me. I could finally relax. He was in charge, and I could follow his lead, instruction by instruction, step by step. And where was he leading me? He was leading me to the solution we both had in mind—exactly where I wanted to go.

During those two weeks we discovered that we could communicate and codream. We could reach outcomes together. And through our voices we could feel something more—an energy flow that wasn't usually there, an ease that was compelling and attractive. Once we had stepped out of the Professional Box and were not confined by our roles, we began exploring the rest of what made our connection so compelling. And we began speaking other voices as well.

Shielding His Lead Singer from Fears and Uncertainties

Whether you are solving a problem or introducing someone to a new business or a new energy source, you will need to look out for his or her safety before you can expect productivity or creativity.

After years of playing drums for top bands, Jerry dreamed of starting his own recording company, producing bestselling CDs and winning his own awards. He sold his dream to his father-in-law, who put up the money. He sold his dream to his wife and kids, who wanted him home instead of touring the country. And he sold his idea to five band members, who agreed to invest two-hundred-plus hours in his dream, now their dream, with no salary.

But after the first recording session Jerry was ready to write off his lyricist-singer. He felt she complained excessively, and he simply didn't want to hear it. What were her complaints? She hated flying and driving an unfamiliar rental car in an unfamiliar city. She felt uneasy in the motel where she was staying. She didn't want to eat the food the rest of the band snacked on during their long days in the studio.

Jerry had never been a leader before, so I explained that in the Start-up Stage of Leadership you are responsible for your team members' physical and emotional needs first and foremost. With that in mind, when she flew in for the next recording session, Jerry shifted his approach. He arranged to have her picked up at the airport instead of expecting her to drive an unfamiliar car in an unfamiliar city. He made sure that her hotel room was safe, sunny, and pleasant and that there was a pool where she could relax and fine-tune their lyrics. He asked about her food needs and carefully met them. Bottom line, he made sure she was comfortably shielded so that she could put her time and energy into production and creativity, into lyrics and singing them. Then her mood and his started to climb. She wasn't a chronic complainer; she was simply in First Gear. She needed to feel comfortable and confident before she could crank up into productivity and creativity.

Corporate leaders constantly tell me that when employees are having problems at home with spouses or kids, moves, fires or disasters, mortgage companies and credit cards, separations and divorces, illnesses and deaths—when their First-Gear needs are incomplete—they cannot perform in Second and Third Gears. Women have risen to prominence as managers because they instinctively take time to make people safe.

Shielding Experiments Before Competitors Can Bury Them

When new technologies are developed, they must be shielded from Second-Gear competitors who would use their power and dollars to destroy them. In 1989, University of Utah chemists Martin Fleischmann and Stanley Pons announced a revolutionary breakthrough. They produced a nuclear reaction at room temperature—on a laboratory table, without any radioactivity—using "cold fusion." If thermal energy coming from these harmless reactions were made commercially available, it could power cars and electrify cities, they proposed.

Within a month, proponents of hot fusion claimed they were unable to replicate their process, citing the experiment as a "possible fraud," "scam," and "scientific schlock." The U.S. Department of Energy (DOE) convened a panel of mostly "hot fusion" scientists that seemed to nail the lid on the coffin. But soon positive observations of the Fleischmann-Pons Effect were coming in from the Stanford Research Institute, Los Alamos National Laboratories, and the U.S. Naval Weapons Research Lab.

Respected British new-energy researcher Harold Aspden, formerly IBM's European patent director, commented: "The hot fusion community was beside itself, outraged at the audacity of such a prospect. There was a conflict of interest, tempered by disbelief, and so we have witnessed a chapter in science that is quite shameful, besides being severely detrimental to our quest to find new non-polluting sources of energy. A drastic shake-up is needed to get energy science back on course."*

Second Gear:
The Voice of the Cheerleader-Manager

The Second-Gear voice has a different tone, volume, and purpose. It speaks about more-better-faster results and how you can produce them efficiently so that you can make money for yourself, and your team can come out on top.

During the first few months of our new friendship, Albert and I spent leisurely hours on the phone talking late into the night and again early in the morning. We wanted to make sure we both felt safe and certain. But the next couple of weeks were hectic, and our conversations geared up into Second Gear almost immediately. Work schedules pressed in on us. Deadlines added pressure. Instead of talking about everything, he prelived his day and I codreamed it with him. And I prelived my day, and he codreamed it with me. Throughout the day we instant-messaged back and forth, cheering each other on and checking on how well we were doing and what else had come up, shifting into First Gear to remind each other to eat or take a break.

The pace of our voices was different in Second Gear—fast, focused, and direct. Subtle details usually noticed were missed. And

* Harold Aspden, "Ten Years of Cold Fusion: Or Was It Ten Years of 'Cold War'?" *Infinite Energy* 4, no. 24 (1999): 15.

we looked forward to shifting up and down at night, to return to safety and certainty, to have time to discover the trail of subtleties we knew we were ignoring, and to make time to discuss the future.

Third Gear: The Voice of the Dreamer—
You Are a "Keeper of Dreams"

In Third Gear you are constantly straddling the crevasse between where you are in the moment and where you dream of being in the future. You need to nurture both of those points by being not so grounded in day-to-day details that dreams are never created, and not so virtual that you dream but never build ways to get there. Like those climbers crossing their aluminum ladder laid over a mile-deep chasm in the ice, you, too, must learn to use the tension between here and now and there. That tension motivates you and gives your life direction. That tension shields you from missing opportunities and new approaches.

For a year Sarah had been trying to get pregnant, and each month she had been disappointed. Finally her mom suggested a new approach—acupuncture and herbs. Her mom went to the appointment with Sarah, and after an hour of taking pulses and asking questions, the acupuncturist outlined a treatment plan and asked Sarah to give him three months. Toward the end of the second month Sarah was feeling edgy and dizzy when she got up. But the pile of pregnancy tests in the trash had all told her no.

One night, just after Sarah's mother had fallen deeply asleep, she heard her phone ringing. Sarah had a hunch and tried one last pregnancy test—and it was positive. She was, to say the least, elated. She and her mom chatted about the baby and the birth, and her mom fell asleep happily nurturing her daughter's infant dream.

The next morning the phone rang early and Sarah's mother heard a voice she couldn't recognize. It was Sarah's; she was doubled up in excruciating pain on her bedroom floor. Her husband was on a plane, and her three-year-old son, Brian, was trying to comfort her. Sarah asked her mom to come immediately. She threw on shorts and a T-shirt, put her dog in the yard, and headed into heavy traffic, calling Sarah on her cell phone midway to assure her she was almost there. Her heart was pounding as she unlocked her daughter's front door, headed for the bedroom, and saw her lying on the floor with Brian by her side. "Mommy has a tummy ache." "I know, Brian," her mom said, "and we're going to make her all better."

Once Sarah felt safe and protected, her executive part reemerged, and she made a series of phone calls as her mom fixed Brian breakfast, got him dressed, and sent him off to school. The first OB appointment Sarah could get was for 2:00 P.M., so they had five hours to wait as her mom helped her into bed and crawled in beside her. They talked and read together all morning. This was sacred time as they shielded the life of her new baby, as they kept themselves calm and positive, never letting their minds wander into the realm of disaster for more than a second before they pulled back to their desired outcome—a healthy new life.

They headed for the hospital and parked as close to the building as possible. Sarah's mom helped her out of the car. In the doctor's office, they waited for more than an hour, continuing to chat and maintain their focus. Finally they were called in, and when the examination began, Sarah's doctor quickly pinpointed the source of pain. Scar tissue from Brian's birth was becoming engorged with blood as the new pregnancy bloomed. And when her doctor scanned her abdomen, there was a heartbeat and an egg sack—not yet a fetus, but definitely a life.

How would she shield her baby during these crucial days? Her doctor smiled. "I could tell you bed rest only to make *me* feel better, but the truth is, if this new life is viable, it will stay. And if not, it will slough away. The best shield you can provide is your faith in a Higher Force."

People Who Shield Others
Also Need Shields

I have been fortunate to spend my life shielding highly successful people and their dreams. I walk through dark places with them. I hold their dreams when they can't. I take calls in the night when they're disoriented and terrified, when their young director or CEO brother or sister dies. And I celebrate their successes with them: overcoming fears and hesitations, speaking up when they've remained silent too long, passing exams and certifications. I savor the rise of their books on bestseller lists and the announcements of their inventions in scientific journals or on national TV. I attend award ceremonies where they receive trophies, including Academy Awards, marriage ceremonies, and celebrations of the birth of their children.

With a smile I remember when they were scared to death; when they were sure they would never make it; when their dream seemed impossible; when they had to take their exam nine times to pass; when they heard their father's voice shouting in their head, "You'll never amount to anything," or their mother's voice saying, "You're wasting your time. Why don't you get a job and stop all this nonsense?"

But "this nonsense" is the essence of who they are, the reason they are here, the part that gets them up in the morning or makes them sit bolt upright in bed; the part that sends chills through their bodies when they recognize connections and make discoveries; the part they couldn't stop doing no matter how many obstacles they confronted. And even if they did stop, that part would just pop up in their minds a year or so later, reactivated by the Razz that never forgets or lets go of a dream.

When Harriet Beinfield, coauthor of the *New York Times* bestseller *Between Heaven and Earth,* started appearing on radio and TV, she was terrified. She was an acupuncturist and writer, not a speaker, and she didn't feel ready. A friend suggested that she work with me. We spent hours walking on the beach in Miami. I pressed her to sort through the information she had gathered to write her book. What was her message in a nutshell? No matter what question she was asked by an interviewer, what points did she want to communicate to her audience? For a week on the East Coast and then a week on the West Coast we crystallized her message and stories. Even then, she still felt unsure about how she would shield herself from nerves and uncertainty. How would she find the confidence she would need to relate to her audience?

Harriet proposed a shielding strategy. Whether she was on *Good Morning America* or National Public Radio she would call to alert me that she needed me there with her, virtually, at a specific time and place. And I would be there, stopping whatever else I was doing and becoming her shield for those few minutes. And afterward we shared.

She could feel me there because I was. She could hear me talking because I was. And she continued to feel me shielding her as she spoke to millions of people.

Success-Filing your shielding successes: When have you shielded someone in your life? When did you speak to someone—your child, a student, or someone who was trying to learn something new—in the voice of the protector? When did you make someone feel safe so that he or she could continue to learn? When did you speak in the voice of the cheerleader? When did you urge someone on and believe he or she could do more-better-faster? When did you see someone going over the top and urge him or her to gear down to prevent disaster? When did you believe in someone's fledging dream with him or her? When did you act as the "keeper of his or her dream"? When did you talk someone through an onslaught of doubt or hesitation or fear? When did you make a person sure that he or she could move ahead successfully? And when did you allow someone to shield you, to make you feel safe and supported, listened to and understood? These are vital successes as you make a change or approach a dream.

When a Shield Is Lost,
a New One Is Discovered

Ana was a top-notch corporate recruiter. Demanding of herself and others, fast-driving and constantly accelerating, she collided in and out of competitive Second-Gear relationships for years. Finally she found a man she wanted to marry, one who was living his dreams and not caught in the rat race.

Ever since childhood Ana had shared her innermost self with only one person, a girl she had grown up with. Ana shared everything with her in person or on the phone. Ana was a Second-Gear warrior: She could tough it out in the workplace; she could shield clients from the ups and downs of the marketplace; she could shield herself and coworkers from overwork and high stress. But she relied on her best friend to be the one place in the world where she could lay her shield down. She never let any of the men she had had relationships with into her heart.

Suddenly Ana found herself bombarded on all sides: a new marriage, a new city, and, for the first time ever, a new job she didn't enjoy. She was making tons of money, but her new position wasn't high-powered enough to suit her. The area of her life where she'd always felt secure now felt insecure, and she found herself reaching out to her friend more and more.

Then the phone call came. Her best friend, her lifelong shield, had been killed in a plane crash. Alone and disoriented, Ana struggled with depression. She didn't know how to cope with the illogical circumstances she was confronting, the inexplicable loss she was suffering, and, given her history with men, she never even thought of reaching out to her husband. So on a friend's advice, she reached out to me and together we began examining her situation with new eyes.

No, she didn't love her job, but her job wasn't what was essential at this point in her life. She had been there and done that, demonstrated this and proven that so many times that she was ready for something else. And a new dream began emerging. Ana was discovering what a sensitive man she had married, how nurturing and supportive he was. Even in her most hopeless moments, he listened to and encouraged her. Day by day she was finding reasons to love him that she had never slowed down enough to notice before.

Little by little she began letting her guard down and allowing him in—and noticing what a wonderful father he would make. Viewing her job from this new perspective made it feel different. If she stayed where she was and developed a team, she would have plenty of time to begin fulfilling other parts of her life. They could get pregnant.

With tears in her eyes, she thanked her lost friend for guiding her to her husband. She finally felt married and she finally felt him as a shield. And together they were ready to shield a new life.

In the Eyes of a Child: "I Love Her Like She's New"

Three-year-old Sam was out walking Sabrina, a neighbor's twelve-year-old dachshund that his mom and dad were taking care of while her owners were away. The size proportion between Sabrina and Sam was perfect as they trotted along together in front of his house. But Sam's mom was concerned. Sabrina had bad hips and try as she might she couldn't keep up with Sam, so his mom stepped in: "Sabrina is old, Sam. You will have to slow down." Sam looked at Sabrina tenderly and said, "No, Mom, Sabrina's not old. I love her like she's new."

You need to be very clear to shield a child. They live in magic already. They see the essence instead of the limits. They love with their hearts instead of their minds. They are operating in Third Gear without First- and Second-Gear foundations in place. As we shield them, we must commit to showing them that dreams aren't just something children have and enjoy. We need to continue taking chances, responding to hunches and instincts. We need to cross that "aluminum ladder" to our own dreams.

In the First Gear of taking action you were afraid of being hurt, made wrong, or abandoned. In the Second Gear of taking action you were fearful of being beaten down by competitors. But in the Third Gear of taking action you must have the courage of your convictions—codreaming and cooperating to make your dream actual.

It Was Finally Time to Meet

After thousands of hours on the phone and the Internet day and night for months, Albert and I were ready to make the long journey from virtual to real, from imaginations and voices to faces and bodies. We were ready to meet; we had a date, time, and place. Now it was a question of coordinating with work schedules and teammates. But when his final okay came later than expected and we went back to book the flight, his seat was gone.

We knew the time frame was tight now, but instead of falling into the crevasse of disappointment and upset, instead of letting go of our plan, we realigned—we decided to find a seat on another flight arriving at about the same time. By instant-messaging back and forth and surfing the same travel site, we inched our way through a maze of full flights, outrageous prices, wrong times, and bad connections, until finally there was a seat that matched our requirements perfectly, even though it landed at a different airport.

In those few minutes we not only got our ticket but also took another leap forward in the process. All through the maze of prices and times we remembered the miraculous and illogical way we had met: a tech-support call I needed to make because I had bought a new computer to use a digital transcriber that didn't work, because I upgraded early to meet my editor's needs, because I called on the weekend and Albert was the person who helped me after seven others had failed. Chance, serendipity, coincidence, or a higher plan—whatever the reason, we had nothing to worry about now, either. At a time when we could have made each other wrong, gotten pushy or negative, we shielded our dream and ourselves and stayed in it. And we knew we could handle those upcoming moments when we would see each other for the first time. Those moments when some of our virtually constructed pictures would have to be reconstructed, when the way we thought we would feel would merge with how we actually felt. And even though we went in and out of fear regularly, we continued inching our way ahead.

The Terror of Almost Being There

As you get closer and closer to your dream, you must remain vigilant. Having Codreamers and Cooperators will be more important than ever. Who else is committed to this dream with you? Who else has done what you are doing or something similar? Who else can you see up ahead who can guide you?

Now you are engaged in that constant last-minute struggle between can and can't, possible and impossible. You're almost there, almost across the crevasse from virtual to real, from having dreams to living them. To keep going, even tiny wiggles and shifts will need to be noticed and realigned. You are ready for the next Success Skill: switching.

Switching Back

N ipping negatives in the bud is what switching is all about—catching and reversing off-course scenarios before they ever start; catching them in the space between thought and creation; making sure you keep your dream in focus until it is realized and enjoyed.

What Does It Take to Reach a Dream Together?

S uccess Skills 1 and 2 are about self-confidence and flexibility. Skills 3 through 7 are about creating dreams and doing the internal and external housecleaning and obstacle removal needed. Beginning with Skill 8, the emphasis shifts to relationship, to shielding teammates as they journey to your dream with you. Skill 9 allows you to align your holograms even more precisely. Switching requires you to pay attention to yourself and others in far greater detail: seeing, hearing, feeling, and preliving exactly what is being thought, felt, and said.

When you're under the gun, how do you relate to your team? Do you take on too much? Do you blame others for not doing what you didn't ask of them? Do your teammates run from you in fear, or do they keep you in the loop? Do you switch the flow of energy away from the dream or keep it directed toward it?

Switching requires you to stay conscious instead of instantaneously and unconsciously slipping back into familiar terrain and old habits. Here are some questions you need to ask in Skill 9: What slightly off-course words or phrases am I hearing as we near our dream? What thoughts or feelings are pulling us in opposing directions? Are we monitoring our approach moment to moment and making corrections? Are we giving and receiving timely and accurate feedback? Are we codreaming and cooperating in such aligned detail that we can guide each other to land not just somewhere but where we want to be?

How Do You Switch?

Instead of asking general questions like What's going on? or How are you doing? or negative-sorting questions like What's the matter? or What's wrong? you need to ask positive-sorting questions that steer you and your teammates back on course: What do you want instead? What can I do to support you? What information do you need? Do you need a hand, or an arm around your shoulder? What do we need to do to make this work? Positive-sorting questions direct your attention ahead to solution instead of back to why not. They point you toward your desired destination instead of away from it.

Finally Marcia received the call she had been looking forward to for months: "Yes, we want you to represent us." Why had a huge broadcasting company chosen Marcia? Because for months, as she flew around the country with their executive team presenting business proposals, when unexpected obstacles surfaced and customers came back with concerns and objections, instead of spiraling down into impossibility, Marcia refocused on their shared dream and came up with suggestions and creative approaches. Even though she had already switched a hundred times, those executives saw her switch again and watched their clients switch with her. Based on what they had observed, they were convinced that Marcia was the person to open new markets for them.

As you close in on your dream, exhaustion and irritation appear just before built-up energy is released by completion and satisfaction—you're like a marathon runner who drags his body over the finish line before he springs into the mad, airborne leap of a winner. First-Gear limits keep pressing in on you—is it right to keep insisting, am I being too controlling? You feel squeezed by the Second-Gear pressures of time and money, quantity and quality—was the job done effectively and efficiently?

Think about what was going on for the CNNfn team during the last few hours before their signal finally came on air. There were those who switched into impossibility and shut down; those who struck out at team members in frustration; those who lost perspective amid the accumulating work stress and pressures at home; those who fell off the ladder into the abyss and had to be hauled back up and realigned. How did the team keep going during those final crucial hours? Their shared dream allowed those who had their wits about them in the moment to switch the others back: "Wait a minute, what do we want and how can we get it?"

You Have to Switch the Point of View You're Stuck In

One of the reasons people go nuts toward the end of the success process is that they get so preoccupied with doing it right and putting in long hours that they lose their focus on the dream, their flexibility, and their creativity. Remember, creativity usually shows up when you're away from your desk, taking walks or showers, driving, or doing just about anything else.

Our sensory system depends on *movement* and *change*. We see things that move. We feel things that change. When we stop moving and changing, our attentiveness and discrimination drop off. And that can spell disaster in the final trouble-shooting phase.

When should you switch? When things start getting hot. When you feel a charge building. When you feel the line overloading. At that point you have a choice to switch your point of view from problem to solution—or to switch yourself off until you can. Like a pilot in a storm, you need to use your point of view, plus all the points of view you can get from the control tower and other pilots in the area. You are responsible for gathering everything you need to land the plane. If you know that you can't land safely given current conditions, you need to divert to another airport and bus your passengers to their destination.

Remember the rules of the hologram: The more detailed the hologram (goal or shared dream), the more power it has. The more parts you see, hear, feel, taste, and smell, the more power and clarity it has.

We are all part of a planetary team. When we can see, hear, feel, taste, and smell reality from everyone's point of view, we will be able to codream and cocreate whatever we need and want. We will be whole.

Commitment: Keeping Your Dream in Focus and Switching Back Again

R andy was producing high-level results in his current position but at a tremendous cost. The First-Gear right-and-wrong work environment he was operating in was exhausting and disheartening. To reach goals at this company took many times more effort than it would have taken somewhere else. Whenever he switched their bureaucratic mind-set from impossibility to possibility, they switched themselves back, heading for safety and control again instead of maintaining their focus on meeting the health care needs of their community. Randy was committed to finding Codreamers and Cooperators. He wanted a pay raise commensurate with the results he produced and enough time and freedom to finally find a mate and raise a family. But like quicksand, the environment he was in was hard to escape from. Without alignment on a well-defined dream, open communication, support, and acknowledgment, he was beginning to feel himself slipping into negativity and hopelessness, too. It was time to move on.

Who did Randy know who was the kind of boss he wanted? Which organizations had the three-gear environment he needed? After numerous calls, breakfasts, and lunches, one of the bosses and teams he wanted wanted him, too. They extended him an offer that aligned with his dream in great detail, and Randy accepted.

But when he presented his resignation, his boss wouldn't accept it. Instead he offered Randy more power and substantially more money than he was currently making, even more than he would be making at the job he had already accepted. Randy was up to his ears in credit card debt and he could quickly pay it off with almost twice his salary. His boss told him to think it over and come back the next morning. Randy walked away confused, as his mind switched back and forth between staying and leaving.

He had already accepted the other job, so he would have to

decide quickly. He had a meeting with his new boss scheduled when he returned from a trip in two days.

But when Randy went in the next morning, his old boss had switched back to his usual mode, pointing out Randy's shortcomings and trying to undermine his self-esteem, diluting yesterday's offer and making its implementation date uncertain. That second visit was like a bucket of cold water in Randy's face. Yes, his old boss had said all the right things in the moment, but that's what he always did. Randy wanted commitment and follow-through. More money would be nice, but Randy refocused on his dream and said no to what he didn't want, and yes to what he did want instead.

What Gives You the Power to Switch One More Time?

What will give you the power to switch from negative to positive, from impossible to possible, in moments you most need to? Bottom line: It's your ability to use the Success Skills you've learned so far.

Suddenly, in the midst of a surgical procedure, Madeline panicked. She was about to pick up the scalpel to do her first appendectomy, but something in her froze and she found herself re-thinking and refeeling times when she presented cases and stuttered and stammered, when she wasn't sure about the diagnosis, when her face turned red and she started losing control and shaking.

But she caught herself. She noticed what she was focusing on and the disastrous results those thoughts would create if she left them in her inner computer much longer. She switched to reviewing times when she had performed brilliantly, more than rising to the occasion, when the information she knew popped up in her brain and she had received compliments from attendings and faculty. And instead of handing over the scalpel and running from the operating room, which she had considered a few seconds before, she felt her hand steady and she performed the surgery expertly, building confidence for the next procedure as well.

You need confidence to be able to switch. Confronted with last-minute doubts and uncertainties, as fear fills your body and anesthetizes your mind, you are tempted to resort to fight or flight. That is the moment when you need to ask yourself: When have I succeeded at something like this before? Success in your past gives you confidence in your future—the confidence you will need to switch from impossible to possible one more time.

Remember, what you think is what you get, like it or not. How long does it take for your thoughts to transform into realities? Have you ever noticed how self-fulfilling prophecies can manifest themselves in just moments? Some experts say we have a fifteen-second window in which to catch thoughts, as thoughts, before they become emotions and actions. Your ability to switch is more essential than ever as you close in on your dream. With next to no time left to create obstacles and overcome them, to clean up upsets and mistakes, having the confidence to switch your focus from impossible to possible, from failure to success, makes the crucial difference.

Which Outcome Are You Actually Pursuing?

When we are exhausted, frightened, stressed, or unsure, instead of heading for our dreams we sometimes turn back and shift down, abandoning our dreams. *Remember, only in Third Gear is your dream actually your outcome.* In First Gear the outcome you most want is safety and correctness. You want people to tell you what to do and how and when to do it. Instead of Success Filing you put your confidence in others and their points of view. In Second Gear your outcome is doing more-better-faster. Your outcome is competition, numbers, graphs, appraisals, and raises.

You are still relying on others' methods, intuitions, and judgments.

As you inch your way closer and closer to your dream—whether one created by you alone or one you are cocreating—and the final rush of "reasons why not" confront you, you will be tempted to gear back to Second: "Forget this dream, I want to do well on this evaluation and get a raise." Or back even further to First: "I want to be safe. I want someone else to take control. I want to know I'm doing the right thing" (the right thing in others' eyes but not your own).

Switch Back to Your Outcome and Try Again

Sometimes we gear back unexpectedly and find ourselves in shock over the outcome we've accepted and now feel stuck with. But the truth is we're not stuck. We can pursue our outcome again, if we're willing to be a bit humble and ask for a second chance.

The day after my traffic ticket hearing, after a couple of sleepless nights with the word *guilty* blazing in my brain and my mind and body replaying that courtroom scene over and over, I got up moved to action and dashed off an impassioned letter to the hearing officer, restating what had happened and requesting a court date. Weeks went by and I had almost written off a response and even started making my no-contest plea right, when I received a notice in the mail that my request had been granted. I could go to court and make it all the way across the bridge to dismissal.

Before entering the courtroom a second time, I spent a few minutes in my car going over what I had learned the first time. I remembered how I felt when I was waiting for my name to be called, when the fear started rising up in me, when that fear drove me into compliance and acceptance. I took time to rehearse a new ending, using those fear feelings as a cue to move ahead: to listen carefully to what was said, to state that I was not guilty, and to present what had happened from my perspective.

Before my name was called, I listened to the cases ahead of me, to the points the lawyers questioned, to how critical the facts were. And when my name was finally called I had even worked through my memories of how angry and fearsome that policeman was. He looked much more docile as he sat there waiting to be called. When he stood up and reiterated the facts as he recalled them, he misstated the date and I noted that discrepancy the way the lawyers had. When the judge turned to me, I told him that I recalled the date to be twenty days later, amid heavy holiday traffic. The policeman quickly corrected his error and the judge turned back to me.

This time, instead of being fearful, I simply said that if I had been the policeman I probably would have issued those tickets, too, given what he saw and what he knew. But as the driver, I had experienced what happened differently. The light was green when I entered that no-left-turn intersection but quickly turned yellow and then red. The cars ahead of me failed to move forward, and I was blocked in the intersection. The only safe choice I had was to turn left. And the judge agreed. Case dismissed.

You will need to be in Third Gear to confidently and flexibly pursue your outcome. Of course, you will still need to use all three gears, but make sure you recognize which gear you're in at the moment and which outcome you actually have in mind.

There Was Even an X in the Sky

Rosalie had been searching for "home" ever since her divorce had forced the sale of her house twenty years before. A few years after that, a Realtor showed Rosalie a house in the mountains she knew was "the one" but instead of listening to her inner-knower, she listened to everyone else. "Why move to Virginia? You don't know anyone there. You'll be alone." She hesitated and stalled amid uncertainty and confusion until the house she knew was hers was sold to another buyer, and she has regretted it ever since.

Recently she started looking again, knowing the condo everyone agreed she should buy wasn't her "home." On a cruise to Alaska, things started to click. A gregarious type, Rosalie decided to ask passengers from California or Oregon where they lived and exactly what they liked about it, and the name of one small town kept coming up: Ashland, Oregon.

After the cruise, she and her friend were planning to drive down the coast from Oregon to L.A., but Ashland was inland. Then her friend chuckled, "Wouldn't it be funny if Ashland was your spot? Let's reroute and stop on our way back. You've nothing to lose and perhaps something to gain."

Just as Rosalie and her friend drove into Ashland, they looked up and saw a plane marking the skies above them with a white billowy X. As she stood enfolded in mountains, as they drove around town, as she breathed the air and talked to the people, Rosalie knew she was "home," and her friend could see it.

But once Rosalie was back in her condo, those familiar voices of disagreement she had been listening to for twenty years started hammering at her again. "How could you leave this beautiful apartment of yours? Are you crazy, packing up and going somewhere without knowing more about it? How much will it cost to move across the country? What a major hassle that will be!" But this time Rosalie talked back: *Hush up all of you! This time I am listening to my dream!*

Was Rosalie being impulsive and reckless, or was she seizing the very opportunity she had been hologramming for years?

As you close in on your dreams, old fears will fly in your face. Comments others make will dash your confidence unexpectedly. Can you, like Luke Skywalker, trust in the Force and keep your dream in focus, realizing your dream will require you to have the same go-for-it attitude the Shoemaker-Levy comet team had when they used exposed film to take their earthshaking photo, the courage Karl Pribram had to explore places current theory didn't accurately explain, and the faith Brian O'Leary had as he ventured into inner space?

Are you willing to disagree with your past, conventional wisdom and normalcy, the usual and familiar, even your family? Will it be okay with you to be seen as unusual, obsessed, a bit strange, naive, and perhaps even foolish? Are you willing to reach your dream— no matter what? Or will you swerve or turn back?

Tell People What You Do Want Instead of What You Don't Want

It is all too easy to slip into the abyss of argument: I can't. You can't. You don't. I won't. I don't have to. Oh yes, you do! Arguments turn energy you could be directing toward your dream against the very people who are dreaming it with you. Switching allows you to communicate "what you do want" *instead of* "what you don't want." The switching skill transforms arguments into requests and clear communications.

When their marriage began, Laurie Ann was between jobs. Her days were spent thinking up ways to please her new husband. And whenever he said, "Hey, honey, would you . . ." she jumped up with pleasure. But then circumstances changed.

Laurie Ann started a new business and almost immediately it became wildly successful. Instead of early-morning workouts, leisurely trips to the flea market to find amazing household treasures, and enjoyable days spent displaying her new finds, things started moving out of her store faster than she could replace them, not to mention the other demands of increasing daily sales and planning a second location. But when she arrived home exhausted, she still heard her husband chanting, "Hey, honey, would you . . ."

Whenever Laurie Ann asked for something, he cheerfully followed through, but without being asked, he continued doing what she had trained him to do and nothing more: "Hey, honey, would you . . ." He wasn't adjusting to the change. And he wasn't picking up the slack. With supportive friends coaching her, Laurie Ann realized she would have to switch her thinking—and his. They were trying to get pregnant and so the responsibilities of pregnancy, birth, and infant care would soon be added to their list.

Instead of instantaneously and unconsciously saying yes, she began taking an extra second or two to think through her answer. When she thought about saying, "Sweetie, remind me to put the wash in the dryer," she stopped before she spoke and switched to "Honey, would you put the wash in the dryer for us so we'll have clean clothes?" She was willing to switch in the short term so that they could love each other in the long term.

Stay Focused on What You Want Now Instead of What You Didn't Want Then

Instead of defending and fighting or sitting on opposite sides of the table, you need to join your partner and sit across from the problem. Switching is changing your mind and positions as needed to reach your dream.

Instead of wanting to know her husband's dreams, Paula got angry at the very first mention of them. Then Murray would clam up, leaving their future fermenting and unsettled. Time after time, she slammed the door in the face of discussion or negotiation. Now they were rapidly approaching a deadline when vital decisions had to be made about where and how they would live. Left to their own devices, they weren't getting anywhere fast.

Based on her past (which she still needed to update), Paula was afraid of being controlled if she listened attentively. As a child, when she listened to her father, her father got her outcome but Paula didn't get hers. Afraid that the pattern would repeat itself, she refused to listen attentively to her husband, barricading herself off not just from him but from their shared future. Murray had been labeled a "whiner" as a boy. Perhaps he was actually a negotiator-in-training but his parents didn't realize it, so he learned to clam up. With Paula in attack and Murray in shutdown, they were unable to negotiate a solution without help.

Murray was a contractor, and Paula had often told me how much she respected his ability to discover his clients' needs and create plans that not just met them but went way beyond them. His clients consistently raved about how profoundly satisfied they were. So, with that information in mind, I switched the way they were viewing the situation from personal to professional: "Murray, what would you do if you had a potential client who got angry as soon as you asked what she wanted, before she described the style and details she had in mind, before she provided the information you needed to interface with building codes? What if she stormed out without ever journeying through the codreaming process with you?"

"I would have to tell her I couldn't work with her," he replied. "Without knowing her preferences, without interacting and aligning on *what, why, where,* and *how,* my creative process wouldn't engage. I wouldn't percolate when I was driving. I wouldn't wake up in the night zinging with possibilities and angles. I wouldn't arrive at a solution we would both be excited about."

As Paula listened to my questions and heard Murray's answers, she switched her approach. Instead of confronting "her father" as a child, instead of being the angry, withholding client, she put on her "contractor hat" and asked her husband to share as many details as possible about his dream, to spell out his concerns and hesitations, to help her understand his preferences and possible solutions. Then a bit shyly, she told him that she had heard everything he said all along, but she didn't know how to *intermingle what he needed with what she needed.* Murray said that was fine. "Now that you've *heard* me, I know the solution will emerge."

We must trust that when all the pieces are laid out, they will find their place. And we must shield ourselves and our Codreamers until then.

Ask for the Support You Need

You are almost across the bridge between virtual and real, almost beyond the chasm of abandoned dreams and disappointments. But the smaller the gap, the more pressure you feel.

As you zero in on dreams, do you get the support you need from those around you? Or do you send out inaccurate messages that prevent their support from arriving?

Marlene and Keith were high school sweethearts who had recently reconnected on the Internet and reignited a spark. They had just spent a week together in New York—one of those discontinuous moments when it feels like not a second has elapsed since the last time you were together. But now they were back in their usual worlds, in different parts of the world.

He was cranked up in Second Gear to make up for the time he had taken off to spend with her, buzzing from city to city seeing clients who had been waiting. He E-mailed Marlene that he'd had a wonderful time with her and he was happily back to work.

Instead of letting Keith know that she had opened up so wide to him that she was having a hard time fitting back into her skin and she needed his help—a virtual hand outstretched, a few days of extra calls—she E-mailed back that she was happily buzzing along, too. But it wasn't true. And so, when he didn't immediately provide the support she needed, she blamed him instead of switching her I've-got-it-all-handled approach to a more instructive one.

Without that information, Keith didn't know what she was feeling. Finally recognizing why she hadn't gotten the support she needed, she switched, and the next time he asked if she was doing okay, she told him no. On alert, he reached out to her: "Sweetie, what kind of support do you need from me?"

Remember, you are a pilot about to land. Instead of giving no feedback or feedback that fails to specify where you are and what support you need, give the details of your present location—physically and emotionally. Tell your Codreamer exactly where you are so he or she can help you.

You Have to Dream Together to Stay Together

But we don't always catch ourselves heading off course soon enough. I watched Teresa slip into upset and disappointment years ago. I kept hearing about conversations she was having with her fiancé, and their dreams never seemed to match. He was talking about joining the army and living in Germany, and she was talking about going to law school in the States. To my eyes they appeared to be headed in opposing directions, not a shared one they could travel together. And a year later, when she was in law school and he was an officer in Germany, they understood my concerns.

They had gotten so caught in the tracks they were following, in the programs they had constructed before they met, that they continued on those courses. Though their paths intersected briefly, they gradually moved apart. Their engagement was broken, and her wedding dress remained under her bed in a box.

In her next relationship Teresa switched. Once their connection was established, they spent months together dreaming. Where did they want to go in the future? What kind of home did they want? How much time and energy did they want to spend at home and at work? Did they want to raise a family? What were their dreams, and were they willing to dream their lives together?

You need to dream together to stay together. And if old agendas or day-to-day pressures prevent integrating and cocreating your dreams, sadly you will end up apart—or together but torn apart inside.

Will vs. Willingness: Sometimes You Have to Go to the Heart of Your Dream

My birthday was coming, and my daughters both asked me how I wanted to celebrate it. For the first time since they were born, I took time to think through their question and answer it for myself—not to meet their needs. I wanted us all to sit down at the same table at our favorite sushi restaurant. That sounded like a simple request, but I knew it wasn't. After battling our way through the logistical complexities of getting us all in one place at the same time, they said yes.

On the morning of my birthday, Cathy called in tears. She had dropped her kids off at school and was chatting with a friend when her friend's dog lunged out the window and bit through Cathy's ring finger. She was on the way to a hand surgeon as we spoke, with a towel wrapped around her hand and her finger throbbing mercilessly. She had no idea of the extent of her injuries at this point. There was so much swelling that she couldn't bend her finger, and she didn't know what that meant. "Sorry, Mom, but we won't be able to make it to celebrate your birthday after all." In that moment, I was far more concerned about the extent of her injuries than about all of us dining together. I'll have dinner with the rest of the gang, I told myself.

An hour later my son-in-law Steve called to say that Sam had fallen off a jungle gym at preschool and knocked his front tooth loose. Steve, Margaret, and Sam were on their way to the dentist to see if the tooth could be saved. They wouldn't be able to meet me for dinner either, and so I called the restaurant and canceled our reservation.

For a few minutes I danced on the edge of upset and disappointment. Would I allow myself to plummet to the depths, or would I switch to a higher priority?

Just then Steve called me back. "Given our current circumstances, how would you like to celebrate your birthday?" I asked him to order in food so we could sit together at his kitchen table, thankful because Sam's tooth could be saved and grateful because Cathy's surgeon had told her she was lucky and she would suffer no permanent damage. Safe and sound in a different place, at a different table, we celebrated my birthday together.

As you close in on your dream, you must be able to inch right up to the point of upset and impossibility and switch back into possible again, redirecting your energy toward the essence of your dream, instead of turning it against yourself, your Codreamers, or fate.

Success-Filing times you switched yourself and others: When did you catch yourself thinking about *why not* and switch yourself back to what you *did* want instead? When did you affirm *possibility* instead of *impossibility*? When were you able to focus on outcome in the face of unforeseen circumstances? When did you hear voices luring you back to *always* and *never* and yell, *No, not this time*? When did your child start telling you all the reasons why he couldn't be on the team or pass an exam, and you prelived his desired hologram with him over and over until he felt better? When did a friend run head-on into fear or disappointment and try to convince you she didn't want the job or relationship you knew she wanted? When did you agree with *success* instead of *failure*? When did someone call because he knew you would help him look at the positive side again?

And Then Dream the Next Leg of Your Journey . . .

Unlike jobs or projects, dreams never end. They keep evolving and expanding. There is always "what's next."

Darlene had been married for twenty-two years. It was a relationship fraught with control, secrets, and rage. Darlene finally had the courage to ask for a divorce and work her way all the way to one.

But once she was out there in new territory, she didn't know how to handle it. Lonely and unsure, Darlene fell back into spending time with her ex-husband. Then he began a relationship right under her nose; memories of times when he had done that before haunted her, and old feelings of possessiveness reemerged. She found herself driving compulsively to places where she knew he would take this woman—and her new power began slipping away. Darlene could no longer see ahead. Instead she started looking back, not at what had actually happened but at a glamorized version, focusing on good times but acknowledging none of the bad times. Sobbing, she headed for her best friend's house.

Her best friend Lee knew how much power it had taken for Darlene to build her business and complete her divorce. And she knew Darlene's dreams for the future. Together they began celebrating Darlene's life-changing successes and looking ahead to what she wanted on the other side of this frightening chasm. Darlene started to smile again, and two hours later, reoriented and redirected, she pulled out of her friend's driveway in the direction of her dreams.

Once you've reached the other side of the bridge, disorientation is still a danger. When you fail to keep dreaming, you find yourself out there in the dark, like driving without headlights, wanting to turn back to where the bright lights are. To head toward your dreams, you must recognize that you and your Codreamers must continue lighting the road ahead.

You don't head for and then stop at a dream. Dreaming is a process of creating, editing, changing, updating, and redreaming.

The Last Quarter Inch

After we spent months and thousands of hours on the phone, learning far more about each other through our conversations than we would have face-to-face, the day was approaching when Albert was finally scheduled to arrive. Suddenly the pull of last-minute uncertainties started welling up in our minds and bodies. We spent hours switching each other's fears. During those last few days we talked even more than usual, sketching out possibilities and aligning on a plan.

We had met on the phone in the midst of a computer crisis when a romantic relationship was the furthest thing from our minds. But almost immediately something inside both of us knew we had a special connection. We could feel it, and the longer we talked, the stronger it grew. But we were in a professional box, and there we would stay until my problem was solved.

Perhaps, if the problem hadn't been so complicated and lasted so long, it would have been possible to ignore our building feelings. Perhaps we would have missed what was right there in front of us if I hadn't been spending hours a day writing about chance and serendipity, outcome over method, and moving past fears—if he hadn't been courageous enough to finally reach out to me.

Early on I was so afraid of losing what had grown so precious to me that I proposed we never meet so reality could not interfere. Albert chuckled at the very thought of my fear-driven suggestion. "But, Susan, what might we be missing? What unknown opportunities would we be passing up? What if these unrealistic, illogical circumstances were the very ones we must brave to meet our true mates?" "Yeah, but I'm a grandmother," I said. "And I'm Chinese," he retorted. "But I don't care if you're Chinese." "And I don't care if you're a grandmother." Mutually reassured, we began imagining how and when we would finally see each other.

I preferred to meet in my home, and he preferred that, too. It was then that I told him unequivocally I could not pick him up at the airport. Yes, we had exchanged pictures, but I couldn't bear walking up to this man I felt so profoundly connected to and asking, "Are you Albert?" Besides, I confessed, it wouldn't be safe for me to drive in that moment! So he agreed to take a cab from the airport to my house.

A few weeks before we met, Albert reached out to my family.

One of my daughter Cathy's best friends died in a plane crash, and when he heard about her loss, he immediately called to comfort her. She appreciated his outreach and told me how much she liked him. A week or so later Albert and my son-in-law exchanged E-mails and chatted on the phone, and my son-in-law liked him as well. I wanted to make sure my family would be codreaming with us, and they let me know they were. They had seen the twinkle in my eye, and they were happy for me.

Then the day before Albert was scheduled to leave, he awoke to tornado warnings and severe thunderstorms, and his mind began doubting whether he would be able to get to me at all. As soon as I heard the dire scenarios he was beginning to concoct, I gently asked what he would want instead, how he would like his travel day to go. Later in our conversation, he told me that he would be missing a lot while he was away—helping a friend move, attending a lottery at work, celebrating his manager's birthday. And with a giggle I asked him what he would be missing if he didn't meet me?

Seeing Is Believing,
or Is It?

For most people, seeing is believing. But for highly successful people, preliving is believing. They see, hear, feel, taste, and smell the reality they have in mind. Their dream is real to them *before it ever occurs*. That's how they attract results. That's how they courageously step from virtual to real, how they walk all the way across the bridge from dream to reality.

As you close in on your dream, every thought and word counts. Tiny doubts and hesitations, small oversights and confusions need to be corrected immediately, as a pilot tightens his course as he prepares to land. The last quarter inch is another time in the success process when Codreamers and Cooperators can assist each other by observing and switching negative scenarios that appear in their minds and bodies.

Not, but, maybe, can't. I don't want to; I hope we don't; it would be horrible if . . . These words and phrases point up conflicting headings that, if left uncorrected, would take you off course. These words alert you and your partner to the fact that you have other destinations in mind; you are consciously or unconsciously creating other scenarios that split your focus and dilute your energies. You are like forces adding or subtracting from each other. *You must have the same destination in mind to arrive there together.*

Notice which gears you shift in and out of as you read our story. Notice when you gear back into safety or right and wrong; when you gear up into time, effort, and money; or when you shift into Third Gear and allow our story to inspire you to step into the dreams you believe in.

It Was Finally Time for Him to Arrive at My Gate

Our relationship had been magical from the start, and I wanted to make sure our first meeting was, too. We planned to meet in the place where we had spent so many thousands of hours in the virtual world—talking in the dark. We wanted to find each other through our voices. That was how we knew each other. Once we were connected at that level, adding the other senses would be easier. We had sent pictures, of course, but it is always jolting to make the subtle adjustments between what you see in a still picture and what you sense when you meet the actual person.

He agreed to fly in, call me from the airport, and take a cab to my home following exactly the directions I had E-mailed him.

Then, with a twenty-minute window, I would dash about lighting candles and making last-minute adjustments in my home and emotions. He would be landing in a new city, taking a cab in unfamiliar territory, and stepping into my house alone, so I wanted to provide him with as much certainty as I could, short of meeting him at the gate.

I spent the afternoon tying colorful tropical leaves into thirty-two yards of silky golden cord that I had driven from shop to shop to find. I simmered a huge pot of soup in case he was hungry and began baking banana-raisin bread so its aroma would greet him at the door. Filled with tender feelings, I trailed the leafy garland along the floor to guide him step by step from my front gate across my living room, through the door and around the pond to where I would be sitting. Waiting always seems to stretch time, so the afternoon and evening were predictably long. When it finally got dark, I adjusted lights up and down and moved obstructing chairs, imagining as carefully as I could how venturing into my territory for the first time would feel to him.

When he called from the airport, the pace of my heart picked up. I thought my part would be easy, but once the candles were burning and I scooted to my place, it wasn't easy at all. When I heard the cab pull up in front and heard the bells on the gate ring and the familiar creak of the inside door opening and closing, my need to call out to him was so strong that I had to clasp my hand over my mouth to give our dream time to play out, to allow him to meander along the leafy trail, to align what he imagined my world would be like with what his senses were streaming into his brain.

We had agreed that I would remain silent and he would call out my name. Even though I couldn't see him, I could feel him getting closer. Finally I heard his voice and recognized its sound and feel. As he settled down beside me, it was as though we had simply stepped from the virtual world into the real one. It had been easy and seamless. We were talking in the dark. And our reality was even more precious than we had dreamed.

Which Gear Were You In?
Which Outcome Did You Switch To?

Which gears were you operating in as you were reading our story? Were you in First Gear, concerned about our safety, feeling I was wrong for letting a "stranger" into my home, worried that we were setting ourselves up for pain and disappointment? Were you in Second Gear, wondering how much effort it would take to make a long-distance relationship work? Or how much our phone bill for those thousands of hours would cost and what rate we were paying? Or were you in Third Gear, enjoying our meeting with us?

Yes, we had approached our dream from all three of those gears, too. We were both committed to making our meeting safe first and foremost. We had spent far more time getting to know each other than anyone else we'd ever dated. We had rearranged our mornings and nights to make time to talk and learned to cat-nap to keep up with everything else. We had long since acknowledged how much we were investing in our relationship—our phone bills had arrived! We had cocreated our meeting, trying out thousands of scenarios and aligning on one. This was our dream. We had prelived it in all three gears before we stepped into it.

Seeing is believing. No, for highly successful people, preliving is believing and creating.

Who Do You Share Your
Most Precious Dreams With?

Which dreams do you share and which ones do you keep secret, and why? Whose objections are you afraid to include and consider? Whose agreement is more important than your dream? Whose sense of possibility and impossibility do you trust more than your own? Whose dreams are more important than yours?

Albert and I talked about sharing our story with family and friends. Who should we tell, who should we not tell? Some would feel we were wrong. Some would think our relationship was improbable or impossible. We looked at these objections to see if we could stand up to them. Were we wrong in our minds and hearts? Was our relationship impossible? No. We had handled those objections, so having them reflected back to us wasn't a threat. Because inside, we knew.

Then when I wrote our story, the question of sharing it came up again. Were we willing to share our story with you in print? What was our purpose? This conversation added many more hours to our phone bills as we examined it from every angle. And this is what we decided.

We are sharing our story so the dreamer within you will be encouraged. So you will keep dreaming and sharing your most precious dreams with the rest of us. So when an opportunity appears magically, you will be inspired to explore it. This is a gift we are willing to give, a joy we are willing to share.

What Have Dreamers Been Afraid to Share with Us?

What have we never learned because dreamers were afraid to share the details of what they were thinking and doing? What opportunities have we missed because people were afraid to propose their dreams to us? Were they scared we would judge them, or prevent them? What inventions are we not enjoying because we couldn't imagine and support them?

Are you willing to tell others how you reached your dreams? Are you willing to inspire others to reach theirs? Will you share how you reached your dreams with your mates and friends, with your kids? Will you offer team members—employees, contractors, and Cooperators—all the details they need?

We are all dreamers who need to begin codreaming and cooperating so that we can complete our mission of joy here on Earth. Will we learn to trust each other and the success process? Will we openly talk about our fears and objections so that we can move past them? Will we freely share our intuitions and new methods so others can use them, too?

Again, I want to thank the people who let me inside their minds, hearts, and emotions so that I could discover these Success Skills. Thank you for sharing your dreams and how you realized them. Thank you for the dreams we will all enjoy as a result.

Maintaining
Your Balance

J ust what has been squeezed out of our lives? The joy? Yes,
we have more stuff—appliances, technology and devices,
choices and varieties. We work faster and smarter than ever
before, but what have we lost in the process? The softness and
ease? The thoughtfulness and cooperation? The dreams?

Ever since I was a girl I have loved seashells, especially the
sliced-open, inward-winding, many-chambered nautilus shell I
always kept beside my bed. But it wasn't until I was an adult that I
realized a soft, amorphous, fleshy creature had exuded that shell
chamber by chamber as it grew. My discovery came when a friend
gave me a picture book that finally introduced me to my shell's
flowing, undulating creator. Now when I view a seashell, I see it as
only partial—the solid part created by the fragile, alive part that
had been there but is now gone.

For me, the philosopher Viktor Frankl's poignant observations of Holocaust life have greater relevance today than ever before. Incarcerated in those camps, knowing that death was probably inevitable and perhaps imminent, no one wished for more time at work, more money, or more stuff. What the inmates longed for was more time with friends and family, more dinners around the table, more mornings waking up and getting dressed, more moments when family and community pulled together to help each other through narrow places.

No, it wasn't the hard, cold, shell-like elements they cherished; it was the flowing, fleshy, warm, day-to-day parts of life, the very parts Second Gear squeezes out: missed bedtimes, holidays rushed through perfunctorily under pressure, bedtime stories never read and savored, tender moments of touching and embracing never engaged in—a hand reached for, a shoulder brushed, a wink that passes electrically across a room at just the right moment, when it is needed.

Sitting at the Table with His Parents

There he sat in the restaurant trying to uncrease the sharply pressed crease in the linen napkin on his lap. Another evening out with his parents talking business. As a teenager, he dreaded those long, agonizing occasions. He didn't understand what his parents were discussing, and he was bored.

But buried deep within those conversations was a gift Tarleton would come to recognize only much later. During those apparently pointless hours, his parents were secretly initiating Tarleton into the fullness of the Success Process; they showed him the squishy parts a teenager normally doesn't notice, the parts that create life, its protections, and possessions, generating cars, homes, lifestyles, and, ultimately, Earth-changing contributions.

At the time he didn't realize he was being allowed backstage in his parents' lives, into the producing and directing, scripting and rehearsing, nerves and jitters, disappointments and redirectings. When at another dinner table fifteen years later, with a creased linen napkin in lap, Tarleton told his mother how precious those "previously boring" conversations were to him now, Fran could see he had gotten the gift they had tucked deep inside those experiences—the reason they had brought him along in the first place. Just as his parents had hoped, Tarleton had found *the creator part within him;* he was producing and directing, scripting, rehearsing, and redirecting. He was beginning to exude his own polished shell, one that fit him precisely because he was taking responsibility for creating it; one that would grow chamber by chamber with him.

Keeping Your Balance, the Most Important Skill of All

Some things remain true: "When health is absent, wisdom cannot reveal itself, art cannot become manifest, strength cannot be exerted, wealth becomes useless, and reason is powerless" (Xerophilus, circa 300 B.C.).

As I began exploring success, many people were referred to me. But on closer inspection, not everyone who appeared to be "highly successful" from the outside really was. Many were succeeding in one area at the sacrifice of everything else. Many were climbing the corporate ladder, but their family lives were slipping and falling. Many were successful in one area, but their health was a disaster; their lives were a string of breakdowns and restarts with next to no breakthroughs.

Going beneath the surface, it became obvious that the most important Success Skill of all—Maintaining Your Balance—could only be enjoyed when the other nine Success Skills were being used. As long as people lacked confidence, stayed stuck in any gear or used it inappropriately, were unable to create powerful dreams and communicate them to others, were unable to use other people's expertise or let go of past failures and disappointments, were unable to hold an outcome and shield it from destructive forces, were unable to switch back to possible and positive, they simply couldn't keep their own balance, nor could they savor, and pass on, the joy of success.

What has been tucked deep within this book all along has been the tenth skill. To maintain your health and balance and rebalance our planet you must develop a broad view of the Success and Leadership Process and its shifts and changes—a sense of life and its subtleties and nuances.

Highly successful people use each skill as needed, and they use them so seamlessly that it's challenging to see when the transition from one to the other is made. The tenth skill is knowing *when* to use each skill.

Like a dancer developing a feel for the dance, learning to transition from one step to the next, to sense the rhythm and flow, you will need to use these skills over and over until they become yours. Until you, too, find yourself using them so seamlessly that you're unaware you are using them at all.

Skill 10 is the joy of success. The ecstasy of leading our lives . . . skillfully.

Approaching Your Goal in Third Gear May Be Unfamiliar

It may feel uncomfortable as you near your goal in Third Gear—it's too easy; you're getting too much sleep; you're too flexible and creative. What's wrong? you might ask. But nothing will be wrong. It will simply be unfamiliar, unlike the panic you are used to in Second Gear. The heart-pounding fear, stress, and exhaustion will be missing. The frenzy of pushing so hard you can't think straight won't be there. You may not feel like you're giving your *all*—and you won't be. You will still have energy to relate to and nurture yourself and others. You will still be able to use feedback and intuitions instead of slipping into automaton mode where you simply crank out more and more of what isn't working or wanted.

You have probably been conditioned to believe cramming is good, all-nighters are necessary, exhaustion and shaking are intrinsic parts of getting close to an exam or an interview. But they aren't; they are simply symptoms of being stuck in First and Second Gears. You can go much further when you pace yourself; you rest and nurture yourself and others. You can move beyond imagined limits and journey all the way to your dream. You can begin experiencing the joy of success.

We must make time for ourselves and our partners for relationships to remain intimate. Otherwise, guarded and protected, we quickly gear back to childhood issues, to arguing about right and wrong. If we give our *all* at work, we will not only *not* have anything to give but also actually begin taking energy from the people who are most committed to nurturing and loving us. If we fail to say yes and no appropriately, we will find ourselves alone at the end of our dream. And that success will feel empty with no one to share it.

Where Does Planetary Balance Begin?

I remember the morning I walked into the pitch-dark amphitheater at the University of Massachusetts and saw huge images of planetary disease—trash in once-clear waterways, dead fish on dirty rivers, children starving and dying crops—projected on the wall in front of us, leaving us disturbed and breathless. What havoc are we wreaking as we manufacture and consume, as our society spreads its consumerist point of view around the rest of the world? How will it affect our health and balance—and our planet's?

Planetary balance starts with you; it starts with balancing your life.

Before we can reestablish environmental balance, we must take a look at our own lives. Where are we misusing ourselves and the people around us? Where are we raping and pillaging our resources and support systems, pushing past recyclable limits, and ravaging our health? What are we overlooking that at a holographic level is exactly the same?

With these ten Success Skills in our hearts and minds, we have a choice. We can continue to operate as though the cold, hard, shell-like remains *are* who we are—our homes and cars and buildings and roadways, the remains we are leaving for archaeologists to find, all the indications of life but *not* that life itself. Or we can begin to explore and honor the squishy creature that resides within that shell, the creator of all that; the creator who longs to make a difference here on Earth, who loves his or her family and friends, who responds to the seasons outer and inner, the hot times and cold times, the dry times and far too wet times. Who is that creator? And how does that shell reflect something much more profound—human life?

Yes, that shell is important, just as food and safety are essential. But why does that creature exist? What difference can it make to itself and everyone else on this inward-winding, ever smaller and smaller planet we call Earth?

I Know
That I Know

To me, success is something more nurturing, more subtle and quiet. It goes beyond the physical and the ethical, beyond my genetic family to the family of man, beyond my identity to the whole, to moments when *I get it. Aha, that's what that meant.* To times when I simply know that I know.

My journey is a spiritual one; my struggles created by the higher part of Who I Am so I can grow and expand into more and more chambers. So I can weed through old assumptions and decisions. So I can find peace and inner perfection, moments when I know it's as simple as *I am safe in my universe. I am a Cocreator.* But then there's a roof leak, or an urgent call or E-mail, or I cut my finger gardening and I downshift appropriately to keep myself in order in all these realms, like a juggler.

And I regularly enjoy magical days, when I think about wanting cuttings of a red spiky flower and a tenant for my apartment, and minutes later my neighbor—whose fuzzy, black dog has been dragging him over to me to get morning hugs for years—finally invites me to see his garden before he moves in a few weeks. And there in his backyard is exactly the red spiky plant I was just wanting and he offers me all the cuttings I can take. And as we talk more, he tells me his house sold more quickly than he expected and he desperately needs to find an apartment in this area. And, until that very moment, he didn't know I had one, much less that it was available immediately.

Magic, intuition, guidance, whatever you call it, that's how I met Buckminster Fuller; how I brought my Success Skills into American Express, The Upjohn Company, and CNN; how I bumped into my video producer, my agent, and my publisher. And, at the end of this long string of way beyond First- and Second-Gear coincidences, this is how I have come to meet you and pass on these skills. It's the magic of a dream, and now we are beginning to understand that—believe it or not—it is scientifically provable.

Chance
Happenings

Acknowledgments

AND BIZARRE

CONNECTIONS

The process of getting this book published and out to you began when I laid an early copy of the manuscript on a bench in a locker room and someone I barely knew asked, "What is that?" and handed me a scribbled note with the name of an editor. Teresa Lee Oster has been there for me ever since, idea after idea, pressing me harder and harder to go deeper—never more than a phone call or an E-mail away.

Patti Pitcher initiated another long string of connections. She has long believed in my mission and called me after a couple of years' silence to ask what was happening with my book. I told her I was looking for an agent, and she made a call. The next day I heard from Tanya McKinnon in New York. Within days she was a believer, too, and when Tanya believes in something you can expect action. After months of fine-tuning our proposal, a joint effort between Tanya, Richard Simon, and me, she delivered it.

The very next afternoon she called to let me know that a Harper-Collins editor was interested. How did that happen so quickly with the editor out of town? Her associate saw the proposal on her desk, opened it, and got caught up in reading it. Excited, she called Joanne Davis to let her know this was "a hot one"—she should read it immediately. But the chance happenings and bizarre connections didn't stop there. Within months Joanne decided to leave HarperCollins and passed my book on to another editor who had read it initially as well. Henry Ferris gave me a call and let me know he was a believer, too. After reading the rough first three chapters, he gave me free rein to keep going full steam. And we were under way together.

As the August deadline grew near, my team expanded further. Not only did my clients, friends, and neighbors volunteer to come in and read chapters out loud so I could hear where they hesitated or had questions or comments, but I had a countrywide E-mail team of Codreamers as well. Teresa was there, always egging me on past comfortable limits. Leslie Ehrin made sure I kept the pace moving. My friend Harriet Beinfield made it richer and deeper. The people whose stories were included kept in contact, too, eager to share their hard-earned realizations with you. Mara Reuben's business savvy kept me speaking to that part of my audience. She was always there to read out loud to me on the phone, to swap daily challenges and triumphs. Thanks to George Cole, my acupuncturist, for keeping me healthy and energized. To Myles Starkman for chiropractically undoing what so many hours a day at my keyboard were doing.

My daughters were there, too. My hardest critics and greatest supporters, they were never afraid to challenge or penetrate more deeply into what I was saying. Near the end, my daughter Margaret read a tame version of the introduction and, sitting at her kitchen table with tears welling up in her eyes, urged me to tell you about the dark times, the times she saw me as courageous. Cathy has always been my cheerleader and promoter. She used these skills to climb to a top position in medical sales and then gave it up to be a mom. My grandchildren Dylan, Eliza, Sam, and Marc constantly provided stories and reminders of how early these skills can be learned. My daughters inspired me as I watched them parent. They have so profoundly integrated these Success Skills that it is hard for them to see them anymore. They grew up with them. They are part of them. My thanks to my sons-in-law for their power as individuals, husbands, and fathers. I am profoundly happy with the family we have cocreated, and for the way we use these Success Skills every day of our lives. To my beloved friends John and Sharon who reminded me that joyful relationships come when you least expect them.

And to Albert for renewing my heart.